PROVERBS 31 Woman

More Than The Good Wife

CARLA B. GEORGE

Published by BermudaConnect

ISBN 13: 978-0-947481-17-9
ISBN 10: 0947481176

Cover Design: Christopher Thomas
Interior Design: Brandi K. Etheredge
Copy Editor: Yvette Blair-Lavallais

Table of Contents

Acknowledgments

I really feel like this project sent me into an outer body experience. I had never imagined I would write a book and can only attest to God's intervention in my life and providing me with the words, insight and tenacity to complete this book especially for you. I do not take such a task like this lightly. My faith has increased and my connection to God is even stronger. I am forever thankful to my Creator and Savior.

To my dearest, best friend. The one I prayed for and who was created just for me. You have tarried with me and endured my late nights and early mornings. You have been an encourager always supporting me with your prayers and continuously speaking over my life with such conviction. If I didn't believe in me you surely did! My husband Marcus, I love you and I love us!

To my parents Wendy and Carlton Lambert who have always believed I could do anything I put my mind to. The prayers of parents are evident when you know your life could have turned out differently if God didn't extend His grace to them by keeping me. I thank you and love you for always showing unconditional love towards me.

To my book coach Gaynete' (Edwards) Jones thank you for the push and ensuring that this book was birthed. To my editor Yvette Blair-Lavallais, I thank you for your honesty, encouragement and excitement that reaffirmed God's purpose for this book.

And to my Mt. Zion Church family, my dearest friends and my support systems who journeyed with me, prayed for me or held me accountable not even understanding the timeliness of your encouraging words. Friendship is family to me and you are the extended family that I love dearly.

Introduction

I remember as a child I was fearless. I could be shy in certain circumstances but any task I was challenged with, I knew I could accomplish it. School and sports came easy to me. In my mind I just knew I could do it. I was operating at close to a 100% confidence level. Making friends was easy and my family was very close. But then something happened. Yeah life happened. See life has a way of changing you and your circumstances. It was once your best friend, but along the way there was a misunderstanding, or a fight and life stopped speaking to you. Stopped encouraging you, stopped supporting you, started berating you and underestimating you. Started sharing your secrets and revealing your insecurities. Asking you 'Who do you think you are?', while at the same time taking you for granted. Year after year that level of confidence is downgraded to eighty percent, fifty percent, then to a mere thirty percent. At times you find yourself failing at life.

I love when celebrities are asked the question what advice would you give your younger self. Man, I would have a mouthful for her! Like yes, you are all of that but not just for you but those who will come to love you. Let down your guard. You are loved even if it doesn't seem like it. Keep that work ethic and tenacity; it will take you much farther in life at a more rapid rate. Remain true to who God made you to be...fearless, beautiful, confident, caring, loving, supportive, giving, adventurous, optimistic, and radical. Yes, live on purpose and as loud as you want. Your strength is needed. You are needed. Shrinking to let others shine is noble but the best of you is needed. 'Would a man rob God?' To be less than His calling on your life is highway robbery.

It's amazing how people view you when you have an opportunity to tell them a part of your story that has impacted your life in such a way for you to change. For me, it was being disrespected too many times in the workplace and in personal relationships.

I gave a Bible study lesson once on *"Faith It to Make It."* Here I told a group of women how I had been struggling in a toxic environment at my job. Ironically when preparing for the Bible study, I thought my story was going to turn into a Joel Osteen, feel good, breakthrough testimony. I was sure that I had suffered enough, and that God's *impeccable* timing would allow me to share with the women about this amazing breakthrough that came at the eleventh hour. But it wasn't anything like that. In fact, my situation seemed to get worse and I felt like I had failed. How could I present a study on faith when I myself was struggling with it? But that's the great thing about sharing and teaching...the message ends up being more for you than your audience. So here I am telling my story of how I was unhappy, at the brink of making a drastic move like quitting my job. Heck I did it before and God sustained me so why not do it again? I was going through the battle and on the front line, if you like. Not everyone gets to hear about the storm when you're actually going through it. It's always the after story or the testimony and here I was exposed, sharing as I was battling. At the end of my study one of the pastors of my church matter-of-factly said, "Well here I was thinking that you had it all together. That your life was all worked out." She continued and said, "You never really know what people are going through." No, you don't, and people go through so much at various points in their lives, which I like to call character-building opportunities.

As I delve deeper into the character building journeys, I hope you can relate. I started a journey of bettering myself and 'becoming a better me' about ten years ago. This turned out to be more of a spiritual and self-reflective journey. My initial steps toward bettering myself started out on an educational path. I thought of the courses and certifications I would obtain to solidify my credibility in my career and any other venture I would pursue. Along the way it became very clear that bettering myself exceeded my capabilities but would need to include character-building moments that would develop my whole being. I still work at it every day with some hurdles in between. The journey should be an ever-evolving process as we should never be satisfied of where we are when God has not yet revealed our full potential.

Along the way I had to surrender my talent, my thoughts and time to God. I had to allow Him to pull some things out of me that I didn't even know I possessed. I had to get rid of some old habits, self-sabotaging behavior, self-doubting and negative vocabulary. What I thought as merely insignificant abilities, only God could take and multiply beyond my greatest imagination. This is His plan for all of us. As you may imagine it was a struggle fighting flesh with the spirit. For example, writing this book was not on any bucket list of mine. It was definitely downloaded into my spirit directly from God. I was completely pulled out of my comfort zone. I was stretched and had to remain seriously committed until the time of execution. It required that I rely one hundred percent on God from the writing, to choosing my book coach, the editor and designer. What pushed me was the thought of failing God. I had to push past the fear of thinking of my personal failure and recognize He provided me with this gift, and never seeing its full potential realized would have been one of my greatest disappointments in life.

When we are serious with where we want to go in life, we have to be serious about where we currently are. We have to be serious about allowing God's power to manifest in our lives so that we can be completely authentic to our calling. We are made in His likeness and *He is the Great I Am*; therefore, we have to declare those things that we are and rebuke those things that we are not. The sub headings of each chapter of this book are intentional declarations of *'I Am'* for you to meditate on and apply to your life. I examine each verse of the Proverbs 31 Woman, beginning with verse 10, and ending with verse 31, from a unique perspective concerning the modern-day woman. I use many of my experiences and those of others that illustrate how we can apply these basic principles to our lives.

I pray that something you read will not only cause you to self-reflect, but also transform your life.

CHAPTER 1

Proverbs 31:10

"Who can find a virtuous and capable wife? She is more precious than rubies."

I AM...
CREATED TO BE MORE

Attending a wedding many years ago, I recall the remarks on behalf of the bride and groom. It was stated over and over that the bride was a virtuous woman and her groom was blessed to have found her. I had heard the term 'virtuous woman' several times when referring to a wife or a mother, and since I was neither, I never really felt it applied to me. In fact, when I took the time to read Proverbs 31:10-31 I did not feel I could even measure up. Though I was a Christian, I felt I was too far gone by committing many sins to be viewed in such a virtuous way. So, I admired the bride at the wedding and accepted that that would never be me.

Time had passed and the thought about being a virtuous woman would cross my mind, but I still felt I could not meet the standard. Well that was until many years later when it was my time to consider marriage. But again, those thoughts took over me...I did not measure up. It was just too late...or was it? If I listened to society then the answer was an undeniable yes! But if I listened to God it was an unequivocal no! I was looking at 'her' the wrong way. In studying and applying all twenty-two verses, we see that though this woman was an amazing wife, that's not all she was and definitely not all she was created to be. She was created to be so much more. When you really stop and think about it she wasn't always a wife and she didn't become amazing when she became a wife. It is written *she was found.* Found already virtuous, in all her greatness and her honour, when single, when childless, when employed, when unemployed, when going through the uncertainties of life, when being praised, when feeling inadequate, when insecure, when dejected and rejected, when betrayed, when loved and unloved and when she experienced that breakthrough! Yes, at every step of her life, even right now. You are amazing right now during this walk – even in your missteps. Every moment always brings you full circle to God's plans for your life.

This woman was so amazing that she was described as being more precious than rubies. Research reveals that rubies are part of the precious stones family. While we usually think of rubies for their beauty as birthstones and treasured jewelry, rubies also have another very specific use: research shows they were laid at the foundation of several ancient Asian buildings as a symbol of structural stability. Being compared to the ruby is not by mistake. As women, we need this reminder that we are the foundation of our families and communities. To expand on this further, the Proverbs 31 woman understands that her role in the family and community extends beyond being the good wife and mother. She is also a successful entrepreneur, a respected woman in society and one to be reckoned with, and as stated, she was all of this before the ring, saying I do and changing her last name. She is all of this because she is Woman.

Understanding our importance to the family unit and overall community will help us to look at ourselves as the regal queens that we are...and then ladies, others will have no other option but to view you in the same way. So, we start. Women ask yourselves: are you making yourselves a precious and valuable find? Anything inexpensive or cheap or invaluable is available to everyone; yet anything worth having and is valued takes effort to find, obtain and keep. In the material world, most valuable things are guarded and protected. There are limited editions and once it is gone you have missed out. That is how it should be with us. We should be regarded so valuable that a man will seek us out and pay whatever price it takes to be with us. And no not financially, but through sacrifice. Sacrificing other women, sex, misogyny, and egos. They will know when they have found a limited edition and will not want to miss out.

But wait... I want to pause here to make this clear. Being a woman is not about winning a man or finding a man or winning people. It is about being the woman God created us to be. That may not include a man, may not include that best friend, or having children, that ideal job or ideal situation, but it does include something much more valuable, and something more precious than rubies – and that is being in a right relationship with God, serving others and most of all loving ourselves. We tend to miss that last point of loving ourselves because we may not have realized our own value, choosing instead to value the opinions of others. When we begin to understand that who we are as a woman is about being the woman that God created us to be, we find our decisions are not based on the opinions and approval of others. Let us be reassured that it's never too late to learn and then learn again. To learn that the standards that define us are not of society, social media and others, but they are standards set by our Creator.

Remember, to be anything other than what God has called you to be is being less than your best. We must turn our ear to God and the things He says about us. Turn our ear away from the naysayers, negative influences and temptations. My prayer for you is found in Ephesians 1:8 of The Message Bible: "I ask – ask the God of glory – to make you intelligent and discerning in knowing him personally, your eyes focused and clear, so that you can see exactly what it is he is calling you to do, grasp the immensity of this glorious way of life he has for his followers, oh, the utter extravagance of his work in us who trust him – endless energy, boundless strength!"

TRUSTWORTHY

CHAPTER 2

Proverbs 31:11

"Her husband can trust her, and she will greatly enrich his life."

I AM...
TRUSTWORTHY

If you ask a woman if her husband can trust her, it is more likely than not that that woman would reply 'of course he can.' However, it is also likely she is thinking she is being sexually faithful to her husband. Trustworthiness extends beyond the bedroom. The question in this verse is whether her husband can trust her to enhance or enrich his life. Daily interactions between a husband and wife can make or break that household. Men are made to find a helpmate. To find more than a cook, a lover or someone to clean after them (not that they do not want these qualities as well) especially when we live during a time where men are able and do participate in the household chores. That 'something more' that they seek (and what we as women seek) is trustworthiness, value and enrichment.

Trustworthiness is a character trait that is eagerly sought and rarely found. In order for people to confide in you, delegate to you or rely on you, they need to feel they can trust you. They want to know you can uphold and uplift when they are the wayward family member, the disgruntled friend, rebellious child or struggling man. Remember 'she' is the foundation of the family and the community and people want to know they can look to you in this way. So, whoever the people are we are committed to, or that rely upon us, they need to trust us and know that we add value to their lives. They need to trust our commitment, our honesty and our values. So how do we become this to our friends, husbands, our families and our communities and how do we enrich their lives? We will turn straight to the Bible for guidance.

James 1:6 guides us accordingly, "Do not waiver for a person with divided loyalty is unsettled..." To put this into context, our messages are lost when our words and our actions do not match up. We must be careful so that we are not being two-faced which is a beast within itself comprised of gossip, jealousy and something we have difficulty admitting to – insecurity. I view family relationships and friendships as the precursor for romantic, non-romantic and professional relationships. Our treatment of our family members and friends is a start of where we can rank our trustworthiness with our peers, colleagues, long-term committed relationships or marriage. In whatever way we choose to respond to them during difficult situations and surprise obstacles can determine the loyalty others place in us. If we are unable to apologise for our wrongdoings, our integrity is questioned. If we are the first to spread the private business of a friend to others, then our loyalty is questioned, and betrayal sets in. If given a task that we graciously take on to save face with our parents, spouses, bosses, or to impress our colleagues or find favour with our pastors, and we later complain, then that brings our overall motives into question. If we tend to frequently complain about minutia events, our faith is questioned.

Judas, a primary example of one whose motives were questioned, and who lacked loyalty and displayed betrayal, must have been known to possess these traits; his reputation proceeded him as we read in John 12:6, where he is identified as a thief, yet he was still chosen as one of Jesus' twelve disciples. Ironically these character traits were needed for the ultimate sacrifice to be fulfilled. This leads to the question, "What can you be trusted for?" Never think trustworthiness goes unnoticed and never think you are good at faking it. How you are needed or used by others is a reflection of what your character says about your loyalty. In order for the crucifixion to occur, Jesus needed Judas to be disloyal. He knew he could count on Judas to betray him to the chief priests and scribes who wanted to kill Jesus. Some people you can count on to spread gossip, some to obtain information and some to tempt others. Some people you can trust to not show up in your life or be disingenuous with their actions. In Proverbs 11:13 it states "...but those who are trustworthy can keep a confidence." Relationships thrive on trust and die in the presence of deceit. Trustworthiness doesn't involve only holding confidential information but includes showing up for others, being a great listener, encouraging others, respecting feelings and others' time, of course praying for others and as the title scripture suggests, it also involves adding value to another's life.

The most important role I play in my husband's life is to constantly support him in his work, his role as the head of our household and to add value to his life. It is imperative as his wife that I do not emasculate him, doubt his ability or always try to be the dominant soul (This last point was very difficult especially being single and independent for 37 years). As with loyalty, support and adding value starts many years before we decide to be in any committed relationship. How are we currently supporting and adding value to others? Is our support conditional or unconditional? Do we support friends and family trying to launch a business or advance in their careers? Or do we look down and criticize their efforts? Are we genuinely excited lending support, offering guidance or spreading the word via social media or other outlets? Do we provide solid marriage advice despite the struggles we may be going through or do we discourage marriage highlighting only the negative sides to it? If you are in a position to promote or connect individuals do you hold that hand close to your chest or are you secure enough to provide opportunities that are otherwise unachievable without your help? Do you pray for and with others? I love how Paul directs us on how we can be valuable to one another in Philippians 1:2-4: "Then make me truly happy by agreeing wholeheartedly with each other, loving one another, and working together with one mind and purpose. Don't be selfish; don't try to impress others. Be humble, thinking of others as better than yourselves. Don't look out only for your own interests, but take an interest in others, too."

A REFLECTION OF GOD

CHAPTER 3

Proverbs 31:12

**"She brings him good, not harm,
all the days of her life."**

I AM...
A REFLECTION OF GOD

Growing up, as a child I was constantly reminded that I was a representation of my family name. So, whatever I did reflected on my parents and what they taught me. My actions could either make them proud or disappoint them. A subtle reminder of this was reflected in how our society relates to each other through making connections. When we first meet someone, we like to find out if we can connect with them through their family, place of origin, career or mutual friends and acquaintances. It is very normal for a more senior adult to ask you, 'Who are your people?' (in a very Bermudian way), or if we hear of a 'headline' story whether through conversation, in the news or social media, we are quick to question the circumstances surrounding the person involved. We question who their parents are, who their family is and whether their actions, *good or bad*, line up. If they commit a crime, and depending on their family or circumstances, we will infer that their behavior was either expected or unexpected. If they achieve an amazing accomplishment we will conclude whether that was expected or extraordinary depending on their personal circumstances.

In the body of Christ, we are also a reflection of our Christian family. At the risk of sounding matter-of-factly, we must be conscious of how our walk reflects our families and our God so that when we go into the world, we do so with a godly reflection of what is in our hearts. We should constantly be asking, "Am I an accurate reflection of God?" Are we quick to judge, do we criticize or anger quickly? Do we curse people out, are we negative or act unnecessarily contrary? Do we respond emotionally to situations and are we able to separate the spirit from the person? What do we feed our spirits with the television shows we watch and the music we listen to?

When reflecting on Proverbs 31:12, let's not get caught up on how we shouldn't bring harm to man more than how we shouldn't bring harm to the name of the Lord, our creator. If this remains our focus all else will seamlessly fall into place. Our motives will change and the reasons behind why we do what we do will reflect in that which we do. In difficult situations it is easy to focus on the person who caused us harm or the thing that is not going our way; subsequently our responses are reflected in our attitudes, actions and words. When we have a need to be right and to be noticed this leads to attacking the person and their mishaps without actually addressing the real issues and how it made you feel. In favourable situations it is just as easy to focus on what we accomplished without acknowledging God. Ultimately, we idolize the degree, position, car, house, relationship or spouse. Our motives to do good shift from reflecting God to self-reflection and are ultimately reflected in our attitudes, actions and words. And for the sake of removing doubt, the reflection is usually self-serving and can create a negative situation.

In Genesis, Joseph's start in life portrays this perfectly. Through dreams, God spoke to Joseph about being the chosen ruler one day. Naturally Joseph was excited, but Joseph's excitement caused him to boastfully share with his brothers how God had called him to rule one day and how they would bow down to him. Here we have an example of how our blessing can quickly become our idol and how boasting about our blessings can reflect negatively on God. How is this so? To Joseph the actual blessing and favour became his focus rather than those whom he would bless and who would help him to attain his blessing. His boastfulness brought harm and not good. It led to a rift in the family, jealousy, bitterness, hatred, violence, 'death,' loss, grief. How did this reflect on God? The brothers rebuked this God that Joseph and their father looked to. By Joseph's immaturity his ministry was becoming a deterrent rather than bringing others closer to God. It even ripped him away from all he knew and loved. However, through God's grace, his purpose was still fulfilled, but Joseph learned to be humble and compassionate and allowed his blessing to speak for itself. He learned that the calling over his life would provide the appropriate platforms and soap boxes needed to share how God had called him and why. He readjusted his focus to whom the blessing came from and how the favour over his life was a direct reflection of having God in his life.

Our simple response or reaction to certain situations can affect not only our walk with Christ, but also someone else's. Are we an immature Joseph or the humbled, matured Joseph? Do our words lift up or break spirits? Do our actions match our words? Do we say one thing and do another? Bringing it back to this particular verse, do we bring harm or do we bring good?

MINDING MY BUSINESS

CHAPTER 4

Proverbs 31:13

"She finds wool and flax and busily spins it."

I AM...
MINDING MY BUSINESS

It was the spring/summer of 2014 that my husband, Marcus, and I met and started dating. During the initial dating stages, Marcus was concerned that our relationship would not last due to the demands of his job during the summer months, which required him to be out often. To his surprise, he quickly learned that I, too, had a pretty demanding life as I was heavily involved with my church, job, studying for exams and progressing with my website. By the time summer had come to an end, he knew our relationship would survive. You see in his prior experiences, women were less understanding of his hectic schedule and were demanding of his time. The distinguishing factor was I was busy getting on with life that I didn't have time to meddle in and nag him about his. Ultimately, to him I didn't try to control the situation or him and this remains true in our marriage.

We start to see the business sense of the Proverbs 31 woman revealed in verse 13. She discovers one of her passions, knows she is good at it and finds a way to make a living out of it. She is focused with no time to be distracted.

She has her eyes stayed on the tasks before her. She is confident in her ability, walking in it fearlessly and diligently. I imagine at every opportunity she is talking about her latest project or passion or service. She is finding ways to perfect her skills and herself and when possible she helps others perfect their skills. She is minding her business.

How many times have we heard that phrase, but in a different context? Usually we are the ones telling someone else to mind their business because, well, they are too busy interfering in our life or someone else's life. But this passage is about us. Are we concerned with the things of life beyond our control, nagging God about it or are we remaining focused and leaving our worries to God? This passage reveals we should be so busy with our purpose and seeking out our purpose that we don't have time to be worrying about who is doing what or who is trying to interfere in our business nor should we have time to interfere in anyone else's. We should worry less about trying to prove people wrong and more about proving God right. Of course, in our flesh we do tend to worry about what others think, what they will say, and how we will be perceived. These thoughts, like the venom of a snake, paralyze us when the only approval we need is that of our Heavenly Father. Worrying about those things beyond our control leads to the stresses of life that could be easily avoided.

Focus. That was the lesson I received from this text. Focusing on God. That was what spoke to my spirit. If our focus is on God, then our business is God. The things we pursue and desire for our lives should come full circle to God. Scripture says: "Seek the Kingdom of God above all else, and live righteously, and he will give you everything you need." (Matthew 6:33)

It has taken and continues to take many attempts, failures and obstacles in my life to realize what God is revealing and perfecting in me. I had to learn this the hard way on more than one occasion. When I was chasing the world and not chasing God, I was distancing myself from what was most important in life, and my purpose was getting lost.

After almost a year of battling a toxic situation on my job, I was ready to throw in the towel. For that entire year, I was constantly trying to defend myself and my worth to people. I was allowing other's behavior to dictate mine. I couldn't understand how just only two years prior to this I was blessed with this job and now I was faced with losing it. I saw a bad situation spiraling out of control. Through it all I was praying and fasting, saying I trusted God to get me out of this situation, yet my focus was all wrong. I was doing everything aesthetically to show God that I trusted Him to remove this situation, but did I truly believe that? Clearly not. The lawyer in me actively gathered evidence to show I was wronged. That in itself became a part-time job. No matter how right I thought I was, the situation continued to turn against me. I was hitting a wall at every effort I made. But that was just it. *I, Carla, Moi* was making the effort. I was controlling the situation. I was being God. I was at round twelve of what seemed like the longest professional fight of my life and my physical strength could no longer get me through. I was exhausted physically, emotionally and spiritually. Every avenue had failed me - at least I thought.

On that final Sunday morning, I refocused and knelt at the altar before God. I had a direct conversation with Him, completely surrendering and asking Him to direct me. I adjusted the lens and refocused on who was in control here. I remembered that this situation was not about me. I had to remember God's purpose for my life was to give hope to others. My complaining, my attitude and constantly meddling in the situation did not achieve that. I had to remember that seeking the kingdom of God, not people, and surrendering was the solution. I got back to carrying out the tasks before me, working diligently and focusing on the impossible being made possible through God. Before I knew it, God had answered my prayers but in His way and His time. He had been providing everything I needed to get me out of this situation. His way was far beyond what I had asked for or could imagine and His timing was long enough for me to be encouraged and conquer another character-building moment. Thinking back on the situation, I see that God always had control. I just had to let go, remain focused and mind my business!

EMBRACING THE CHALLENGE

CHAPTER 5

Proverbs 31:14

**"She is like a merchant's ship, bringing
her food from afar."**

I AM...
EMBRACING THE CHALLENGE

I presume that this verse was intended to display the industrious side of the Proverbs 31 woman. When I read further into this verse it was the actual reference to the travelling merchant ships that stood out to me. Merchant ships used to travel the seas to other countries for the merchants to negotiate within the markets and return home with the goods they were able to barter. Working in the insurance industry for the last five years, I learned of how the re-insurance market as we know it was formed as a result of the shipping industry. The merchants would often face challenges sailing over the unpredictable and dangerous seas, many times losing their wares and the investments they put into their journeys. Of course, this caused devastation for the families and communities that waited weeks and months for the return of their family members and the goods that often included food, water and valuables. The merchants however were not defeated by these challenges; rather, they used the tragedies to form a reinsurance industry that is worth billions of dollars today. This is not unique to the insurance market, but challenges and need often birth many innovative solutions.

I do not like conflict, but I wasn't always like this. There was a time I welcomed conflict and was eager to defend myself and others each and every time the opportunity arose. But it was during those times that I was not my best self. As I matured, I learned that not every fight was mine to participate in and not every challenge was a personal attack on me. This doesn't mean that I no longer have challenges (because the Lord knows I do!), it's just that I am learning to handle them differently. Learning to handle them from a place of peace rather than a place of anger, a place of security rather than insecurity and a place of love rather than hate. As with the insurance industry, challenges in our lives provide an opportunity to address a void that will help shape a better version of ourselves. What I mean by this is that there are situations that we may have thought we have gotten past or gotten over or have released until something triggers that unwelcomed feeling and we quickly realize we still have work to do. Therein lies an opportunity for improvement. An opportunity to shed another layer to reveal your true self. Romans 5:3-4 describes it like this: "We can rejoice, too when we run into problems and trials, for we know that they help us develop endurance. And endurance develops strength of character, and character strengthens our confident hope of salvation." These are what I call the character- building moments.

I learned more to appreciate how challenges help to build character when I listened to founder of Radio One, Cathy Hughes's radio station Praise 102.7. She would open the programming with the same effective prayer each morning at 6:00am (EST). In her prayer, she would thank God for different challenges like times of hurt because it provided an opportunity to show forgiveness, and times of sickness because it provided an opportunity to show the healing power of God. This prayer helped me to look at the challenges in my life in a different way. When you assess the situation, and look for a positive opportunity, the burden lessens, and your perspective heightens.

In the physical realm, challenges expose our weak areas. When I would go to the gym, it was pretty discouraging in the beginning stages. A thirty-minute session felt like forever to me. Lifting ten pounds felt like one hundred pounds and a five-minute run felt like a marathon. I was exposed. My lack of exercise and eating right exposed that I was unhealthy and lacked stamina. Clearly, things had to change. However, in order for change to occur, it's imperative that we acknowledge our weaknesses and not be ashamed of them. It's the shame that prevents growth. A story that highlights this is the biblical account of Samson and Delilah in Judges 16. His strength was in his hair, but his weakness was with women. We don't normally hear about his first wife, a Philistine woman that he insisted on marrying because of her beauty, despite her not being an Israelite. She, too, tricked Samson into giving her the answer to a riddle he posed to thirty men selected by her mother to be companions of Samson. We read about Samson's anger. We even read about how he slept with a prostitute, yet we never hear of Samson addressing his weakness for women. This is evident when Delilah tempted him. He did not have the tools to deal with her. His weakness, in the form of Delilah, tortured him and he tried to ignore it, brush it off and told it to go away. Failing to acknowledge what the real issue was and the challenges he faced led to Samson being fully exposed and broken down in order to be completely released.

Recognizing the challenge, the trials, the weaknesses and the attacks for what they are is a step toward complete redemption. Our challenges may provide an opportunity for us to work on our attitudes, jealousy, relationship choices, anger and maturity. I would wonder why I found myself in the same situations over and over again. I would ask God to reveal the lesson so that I wouldn't have to go through it again. Most (if not all) of the times, the lesson was me. I had to work on me. I had to look at my options and assess what I was choosing. So, when conflict would arise, I had to ask myself: do I attack, walk away or pursue in love? When my confidence was challenged, do I cower in defeat, overreact as a cover-up or face my fears as a confident mature adult? When my relationships didn't work out, do I run to a different, yet same type of man or adjust 'my list' and end up with the perfect guy for me, one who was not necessarily the perfect guy for everyone else? In times of sickness do I expect the worst or pray for healing expecting a miracle to take place? In financial strife do I wallow in my lack or ask God to show me the qualities and skill sets I possess or needed to obtain in order to pursue an alternate option? These are questions that help to mature us, build character and build confidence. The way in which we respond either reveals our weaknesses or shows our strength. With this understanding we can learn to rejoice during our challenges knowing God cares enough for us to want us to be our best selves. The challenges expose our weaknesses that are opportunities for God to work on us and for us to rely on Him. And when our weaknesses turn into strengths, they become opportunities for us to minister and help others and lead them to rely on God and embrace the challenge.

RECLAIMING
MY TIME

CHAPTER 6

Proverbs 31:15

"She gets up before dawn to prepare breakfast for her household and plan the day's work for her servant girls."

I AM...
RECLAIMING MY TIME

"Time is really the only capital any human being has, and the only thing he can't afford to lose"~ Thomas Edison

During a House Financial Services Committee hearing in July 2017, Representative Maxine Waters, the U.S. Representative for California's 43rd Congressional District, asked U.S. Secretary of the Treasury Steven Mnuchin questions concerning a letter sent by her to him that he did not respond to. He avoided answering her questions and rather provided accolades and diversions thus wasting her allocated time to speak. She took exception to his behavior and repeatedly demanded her time back by saying, "Reclaiming my time!" She specified, "When you are on my time I can reclaim it."

If possible, we would jump at the opportunity to take back the time we have lost on things, people and situations that were insignificant. We would vow to make better use of our time if given another chance. Conceptually speaking there should be little reason why anyone who has access to a smart phone, computer or even a calendar should not perfect the concept of time management. Twenty-four hours is a long time to complete anything and many things. That's a total of 1,440 minutes or 86,400 seconds in a day. But like with most things in life, it is not what we have, it's what we do with it that matters. It is often said that we do not have enough time, but if we are honest we can admit that we often waste the time we do have. What we do with our time, talent and gifts can either please or be a disappointment to God as highlighted in Jesus's parable of the three servants. "To those who use well what they are given, even more will be given, and they will have an abundance. But from those who do nothing, even what little they have will be taken away" (Matthew 25:29, NLT). We have those moments where we realize time has been lost and wasted for so long because we have not used the time given to us from God. It is time to reclaim our time!

As most people would know in the legal world, time is money. When I worked in a law firm we had to do the dreaded timesheets. Everyday we had to input the amount of time we spent working on a file and doing administrative work. Firms tried to make this process easier with a tool that actually clocked your work. You could turn it on and off with each project you started and finished. If utilized well, this was a pretty accurate method for monitoring your time. I must admit I did not like and was not very good with timesheets. Not completing them daily meant I had to rely on my memory and emails at the end of the week and then I rushed to meet my deadline and input my time. This often resulted in me cheating myself from accurately accounting for valuable time I spent actually doing the hard work for that particular week. But how many of us do this daily in our lives? How many of us are cheating ourselves of the twenty-four hours we have been given by not accurately accounting for it at all? We take for granted our time with sleep, social media, television or doing anything else other than what we must do to live a meaningful life and a life that is toward our purpose. We also waste emotional time and spending quality time with loved ones. Additionally, a slight contrast to this is the spirit of busyness. Busyness tends to take over our lives and is a distraction of the enemy to prevent us from pursuing the abundant life promised to us. It keeps us away from what is important and keeps us away from spending time with God. It is time to reclaim our time!

In this Proverbs passage, the woman gets up early and plans her day for her servant girls. So, she is pretty successful as she has staff or helpers in her house and she cultivates this success with planning and hard work. She is mindful of not wasting time or taking it for granted or filling it up with unnecessary things. Adopting this same concept, how would you plan your day for yourself? If you planned out your ideal day toward reaching your idea of success what would that look like? Would it be full of wasted time or busyness that takes up unnecessary time? Imagine it is just you and God who are responsible for completing this plan for your day with no excuses or distractions - as if you had no husband, no children, no sickness, nothing that could prevent you from completing a successful 24 hours. What gift has God blessed you with, what talent has He given you, what path are you on to lead you to achieving that abundant life?

I challenge you to write out your day in 15-minute intervals. Some of those 15 minutes may make up an hour or more and some may be broken down further to account for eating, for example. The idea is to plan what an ideal day looks like of making strides to accomplish that goal or vision you have set for yourself but haven't completed. Maybe it's an exercise regime, maintaining a healthy lifestyle rather than dieting, learning a new language, writing a book, reading the Bible, creating art, traveling as a family or solo, obtaining a degree, finishing an assignment, rolling out your business, making a major purchase like a home or car. After completing this plan, write all the distractions and realities of life that prevent you from achieving your 24 hours of success. Children, social media, sleep, friends, family, television. Now write what you can realistically cut from your day to reduce the distractions for that one day. Social media, friends, television can be easily removed from this one day. The only way they should be permitted in your day is if they contribute to the success of your plan. Sleep can be managed by waking up earlier and going to sleep a little later if you have not fully accomplished your 24-hour day goal. Children and family are less easy to cut out yet manageable if we are willing to ask for help from family and friends (for example to babysit, collect children, or do homework). Finally set expectations. Setting realistic expectations reduces unnecessary disappointments and interruptions. It is time to reclaim our time!

The purpose of this 24-hour plan is to ensure that you are making strides to meet your goal, even if for one day a week. Ideally you should be making strides everyday and many of you are; but for those times that you may fall off or are not accomplishing anything at all, this plan will give you assurance that at least this one day in the week you have stepped closer toward the calling on your life. My prayer is that applying this plan for one day will transform into daily habits of success.

Habakkuk 2:2-3 (MSG) is your guide: "And then God answered: "Write this. Write what you see. Write it out in big block letters so that it can be read on the run. This vision-message is a witness pointing to what's coming. It aches for the coming – it can hardly wait! And it doesn't lie. If it seems slow in coming, wait. It's on its way. It will come right on time."

It is time to reclaim our time!

**INVESTING IN
MY FUTURE**

CHAPTER 7

Proverbs 31:16

"She goes to inspect a field and buys
it; with her earnings she plants
a vineyard."

I AM...
INVESTING IN MY FUTURE

Scripture teaches us we ultimately reap what we sow. What we invest our time in, the thing we nurture and watch grow will be revealed in our future. This applies to our spiritual and physical lives, relationships, careers and of course, finances. I must confess I struggled with where I placed my focus financially and personally. I guess when the hands of time started to move quickly it became increasingly important for me to reevaluate what my legacy would be. It was not sufficient for me to merely exist and take from this world - not that I was living completely reckless - but there was more I could do. To be honest, there is always more we could do.

A topic not discussed in detail in many of my immediate communities is finances, especially within the church where the conversation about money can be misunderstood. We view money as being a necessary evil rather than understanding the verse that "the LOVE of money is the root of all evil." It's the love of the things money can buy that turn into idols and creates greed, deceit and debt. That stems from a lack of discipline, understanding and self-control. Similar to the church, women have historically fallen behind in financial knowledge and understanding how financial investments should create a path to our financial freedom. If economics, business or accounting is not our career choice, we tend to be even further behind the economic gain. If our salaries and savings do not allow us to purchase assets that will add to our legacy, then we become discouraged in educating ourselves on becoming financially savvy, and financial freedom is even far more removed. To top it off, knowledge of our female role models is limited both biblically and in the world. Biblical teachings and sermons tend to neglect to highlight Deborah as a judge of her time or Mary Magdalene, Joanna and Susanna as women of means who helped to fund the ministry of Jesus Christ. We overlook the female trailblazers who were instrumental in changing the property laws concerning the people of Israel. Legislation set out that property inheritances were bequeathed to the sons of fallen men. It was the five daughters of Zelophehad, who had no sons, who, as told in Numbers 27, successfully pleaded before Moses for their deceased father's land, forever changing landownership being available to women. Even in this verse we learn how our Proverbs 31 woman was financially savvy, conducting her research so she could make an informed decision when investing in real-estate. Our failure to expose our little girls and our women to these amazing trailblazers and others creates a mindset of successful women being seen as an anomaly.

Growing up, most parents wanted their children to have a good education, and land a good job to be able to purchase property and enjoy life. They wanted their children to be better off than they were. This was wisdom as our parents knew it at that time and I was fortunate enough to follow this path. I have to admit, however, that in recent years I started to view my blessing as a burden. This troubled me because I didn't want to appear ungrateful to God. This was one thing that I knew for sure: I trusted God one hundred percent for it and it was one thing that I could draw on as an example of true faith. It was the one thing I didn't worry about obtaining like I did for love, security and peace. However, it was becoming the one thing that seemed to keep me restricted. An attitude adjustment was needed. I had to redefine what my future would look like and what I would do to achieve that. While I knew He was increasing my territory, I had to understand what my territory consisted of.

I had to make the choice to invest in myself and in my community to ensure the legacy I wanted to leave behind. Not everyone has the same vision of what their legacy will look like but everyone has the power to ensure their legacy is secured. This can be achieved through learning, reading and seeking mentorship, and most of all, having a positive attitude and getting rid of the 'woe is me' syndrome. Through these avenues we evolve in our concept of a better future and for me that was a healed community and financial freedom.

It wasn't until I recently read the book "*Rich Dad, Poor Dad*" by Robert Kiyosaki that made me understand my frustrations. It was misguided wisdom. Growing up in a community where property was valued as power, my parents' advice came from a place of empowerment as they knew it. They knew the days when neighbors, friends and family assisted each other with building their homes, and taking care of their children, thereby reducing complete reliance on private services and financiers. Overtime we moved away from this practice and grew into a selfish, each man for his own community. So yes, my parents and their generation were wise in wanting to prepare their children to survive in this world the best way they knew how. Kiyosaki's *Rich Dad, Poor Dad* enlightened my outlook of how I viewed how I should be financially investing in my future. First and foremost accumulating unnecessary debt cannot be an option. It taught me how I should distinguish assets from debt and that we should be using our assets to purchase debt items, but more importantly we should be acquiring lucrative assets as soon as possible. This was my enlightening moment, which pushed me to learn more about investing and obtaining disposable income, applying it to my life and seeking the financial legacy I wanted to leave. But why was this important to me? Because it will lead me to what I viewed as equally important to my future and that was a healed community. It is essential that while we invest in ourselves we make a concerted effort to invest in others. The Dalai Lama says, "to be happy we must make others happy." So here we add on an additional lucrative asset and that is giving back to our community.

From childhood, I have always been involved in my community. Serving as a Brownie, to a Girl Scout, to learning sign language to communicate with the hearing impaired, to serving on several government boards in my country. When there was a shift in our community that led to a decline in the sense of community, I became less concerned about organizations and more focused on personal sacrifice; sacrificing money and more importantly, time. Recently I have become invested in creating strong family units. It was important for me to support strong families and create an environment that includes security, accountability and selfless values. I achieved this with my husband, holding corporate date nights with many couples called 'The Date Night! Series' where our motto is "Solid Families + Accountable Partnerships = Strong Communities." Encouraging couples to have quality time together with other like-minded couples, outside of children and the distractions of life, is vital. Many conversations with other couples shed light on how the stresses of life kept them apart. They struggled with finding time for each other and showing that physical and verbal love that is very much needed in relationships, and more so, greatly needed to be seen and felt by our children. While couples deal with many challenges, this group is not intended to address all of them, but to release some tension if but for a night. They leave encouraged, more connected to each other and wanting more of the same. While the feedback varies, the prevailing comment that makes it all worth it is that couples are encouraged and inspired seeing other couples openly expressing love.

What investment will you make that you, your children or your community can reap in the future? This is the time to invest in your future because that is the one place you are guaranteed to find yourself in the next five years, five months, five days and five hours. You are never too old and definitely never too young to start. Listening to a Bishop T.D. Jakes sermon titled, "*Lord Make Me An Answer*," encouraged me to not seek money, things and people, but to do a self-assessment about my gifts and use all the experiences in my life, especially the bad ones, toward helping others and providing an answer to a problem that needs to be solved. When you link your gifts and your experiences to aide others therein you will start to plant the seed to your legacy.

STRONG

CHAPTER 8

Proverbs 31:17
**"She is energetic and strong,
a hard worker."**

I AM...
STRONG

Consider the roles we take on that are often taken for granted by others and ourselves. We are daughters, sisters, mothers, wives, friends, employees and employers. We often mother children other than our own, volunteer in our churches, schools and in the community. Our duties vary from nurse, maid, manager of finances, confidant, and counselor. We miraculously bear children at pain levels that are next to essentially breaking every bone in your body *(dramatic emphasis here)*. We automatically handle our daily tasks without really thinking of them as work or something extraordinary. We are asked questions we have difficulty answering and we fight many battles while still losing the war. We have managed to break several glass ceilings only to find steel beams. On the sidelines we are cheered on and dig deep to find the strength to push on. We hold on to titles like 'superwoman,' 'girls rule,' and belt out songs like *'This girl is on fire!'*... Yet!

Yet? Yes, yet. Listening to the stories of women who have accomplished some or all of the above, we discover that their stories usually end with: "I'm just so tired;" "I have no time for myself;" or "I just want to run away;" and "I don't know who I am anymore." We are in a perpetual state of exhaustion, living an unsatisfied life while ironically being labeled as the 'Strong Woman'. So it begs the question, "Have we mistaken what it means to be a strong woman?" Have we desired to be so much to so many people and things that what we are really doing is relying on our own strength and not on God's strength? How could it be God's desire for us to be overwhelmed and suffer from exhaustion? Have we lost the plot so much that we have lost ourselves?

Feeling overwhelmed and drained or unworthy and defeated is a sign we are relying on our own strength. We tend to think we are the only ones who are capable of completing a particular task, rearing our children or can be used by God (hmmm). Our perceived strength has a counter effect. Because we rely on our human strength, we leave little room for the power and strength of God. In essence, our failure to rely on God's strength can actually seem like it weakens the power of God. The truth is that God's power can never be weakened; instead, we often don't realize the power because we don't rely on the power. Equally dwelling in our feelings of unworthiness, ineptness, or defeat also weakens the power of God. (2 Corinthians 12:10) When we take our hands off situations, we can truly see how the power of God will work. He wants us to know that the stresses of life are not ours to bear. We are to acknowledge them, understand why we feel the way we feel and move on in peace while he continues to work on our behalf.

I am reminded of my garden that I have in my back yard. During planting season, I work on everything from prepping the soil, to planting, weeding and keeping the slugs away. After months of being extremely hands-on, I notice the vegetables started to sprout and grow. I then become weary and start to take my hands off, but that did not stop the vegetables from growing. While I allowed the dirt and weeds to take over, my crop continued to grow and press through all the mess. They were still growing even when I took my hands off. This is how God will work in our life. He sees us trying and thriving, but He also sees us struggling, getting weary as the dirt and weeds of life start to take over us. But He is always working on our behalf. His power provides us with the strength we need to still grow through it all, even when we take our hands off. He gives us that permission to just be still and acknowledge that He is God.

There is a quiet expectation that we must always be on point, strong and energetic. This is both society's expectations and our own. But this is far from the truth. Yes, we are very capable of doing many things and being many things to various people. However, without understanding that it is not for us to do it all, we struggle physically, emotionally and spiritually. To avoid appearing weak or incapable, we tend to suffer silently or the polar opposite - complain loudly. This is not strength; this is self-abuse. This is even more evident when we are trying to find our place within our families, our communities or scaling the corporate ladder. Labels are easily placed on women. To take a stand against something we are labeled as being difficult. To be confident in our ability, we are arrogant. To challenge the status quo, we are controversial. To set and meet our goals, we are overachievers. These labels are tagged on our backs as we strap an 'S' on our chest; however, our real strength is in our weakness when we surrender to God. This is where we get back on track, start to see the plot again and hand over control to the Creator of our life and path.

We start with setting Godly expectations on ourselves as opposed to conforming to worldly expectations. To the world David was a mere shepherd boy. To God he was a King. To the world Sarah was an old barren woman. To God she was the example of a great miracle bearing birth to great nations. To the world the Cross was viewed as a cruel death by crucifixion. To God the Cross symbolizes salvation through the ultimate sacrifice of His son for all of us. Perception is reality and it is our responsibility to create our own reality by setting our own perceptions.

WILLING TO TRY SOMETHING NEW

CHAPTER 9

Proverbs 31:18
"She makes sure her dealings are profitable;
her lamp burns late into the night."

I AM...
WILLING TO TRY
SOMETHING NEW

Have you ever noticed that adversity or regret seem to arise when fear and insecurity are involved? Either a) your fear and insecurities prevent you from pursuing a thing and you resort to your weaker defense mechanism or b) another's insecurity causes them to fear you and they resort to their weaker defense mechanism. That is what occurred with a man that Jesus encountered, a man whose insecurity kept him in bondage for thirty-eight years.

In the Gospel of John, chapter five we read of the lame man healed by Jesus. This was a lame man who claimed he wanted to be healed, but did what everyone else like him did. Everyday he laid on one of the porches close to the pool of Bethesda with other blind, lame and paralyzed sick people around him. He never asked for help, he never made strides to get closer to the pool. He just laid there with the desire and hope to be healed, but never receiving it. He could have tried to overcome his circumstances but rather he used it as an excuse as to why he could not move to the pool to be healed. Excuses are our weak defense mechanism that keep us in our comfort zone. It is the easy way out, it falsely protects us and is used quite often. However, Jesus came and challenged the man. First, he asked him if wanted to get better and second, he told him to do something new, something different. He told him to get up and walk. And he did just that!

We all have areas in our lives that we allow our fears, our inhibitions or our circumstances to dictate how we will live out our lives. As a defense mechanism we use these as our handicaps, creating excuses that take over. When Proverbs 31:18 speaks of 'making sure her dealings are profitable,' I read this as being intentional with our daily efforts, with our plans for our lives, with our interactions with others, with our thoughts and actions. I read this as overcoming our fears and insecurities so that everything we do will be of good return, will enrich our lives, will propel us into the next dimension. Our insecurities tend to lie in what others think of us, our past, our appearances, our possessions, our circumstances, our intelligence or our need for validation, just to name a few. When they take over, fear sets in, and as stated above, they become our weak defense mechanisms that take over. We make excuses as to why we won't pursue that career choice that makes us happy rather than making us money. We make excuses as to why we can't take that trip that we have dreamed of for fear of the unknown, or why we don't express our true selves for fear of being judged or worse, rejected. We make excuses as to why we remain in abusive, toxic and unhealthy relationships for fear of loneliness. As you read this, reflect on where you want to be rather than where you are. Think of where you will allow God to do a new thing in you (Isaiah 43:19).

As with the lame man there are some areas in our lives that we need to just get up and walk away from.

Being around other people that were also sick, weak or lame made it easier for the lame man to remain stagnant and prohibited him from moving toward his healing and deliverance. He was comfortable wallowing in his handicap. It made it easier for him to feel sorry for himself and make up excuses. His surroundings kept him in bondage. He was in bondage spiritually, physically and mentally. There are areas in our lives that mirror the lame man's life. We become victims of our environment and our weaker defense mechanism of comfort and familiarity prevents us from moving into the unknown. The unknown is where we find our strength, healing, peace, deliverance and success.

The people were so used to seeing the lame man in that sick, lame state that when he was healed, the Jews spoke against it. This was the start of the adversity against Jesus. They challenged the man's healing primarily because he was healed on the Sabbath, but overall they actually feared the change that had occurred in the man. What occurred went contrary to protocol, to tradition, but mostly against the expectations they had placed on him. They were comfortable when he was lame and unable to move forward. They probably wished him well but secretly didn't actually expect him to be healed from his past or his handicaps. They really didn't want him to be better off and definitely not greater than them. Oh yes, when you start to defy the expectations others place on you, you stir up insecurities within them that they were not even aware of. Now they see he was walking toward a better calling over his life. They see him walking in his potential. But when we examine the scripture we realize that their attacks were not necessarily against the man but against the man who healed him. Their insecurities feared He who was more powerful than them and that was Jesus. This is a reminder that when we pursue a different path, the one God has called us to, we will be judged, talked about, doubted, and jealousy will meet us at our doorstep. Understanding the reason behind these attacks we will be less inclined to take them personally.

There are many examples in the Bible where people had enough of the situation they were in and did something new to receive the deliverance, change and healing they needed. Zacchaeus climbed the sycamore tree; the people walked seven times around the walls of Jericho and the walls fell; and the woman with the issue of blood pushed through the crowds just to touch the hem of Jesus's garment to receive her healing. The danger of staying in the same comfortable position leads to stagnation, repeated abuse, unhealthy lifestyles, depression, unhappiness and regrets. Think of where you can let go of your weak defenses and start living out the life God has destined for you. Never limit where you have dreamt of being or what you imagine for your life. Nothing is unattainable when you take the limits off.

PRACTICING
SELF-CONTROL

CHAPTER 10

Proverbs 31:19

**"Her hands are busy spinning thread,
her fingers twisting fiber."**

I AM...
PRACTICING SELF-CONTROL

I have never seen anyone actually spinning thread, but the one image that does come to mind is the story of Sleeping Beauty. While this may not be the most credible reference, it is pretty relatable. We see in that fairytale that when handling a spinning wheel, you have to be extremely meticulous, having a steady hand exercising some form of control. Beauty was mesmerized by this new machine that she had never seen. Without understanding the danger before her, without haste or thought, she could not control herself and walked right into the witch's trap. In her attempt to control the spinning wheel, Beauty pricked her finger, immediately triggering the curse, and causing her to fall into a deep sleep for one hundred years. When I read this, it hit me that it wasn't her lack controlling the spinning wheel that led to her demise it was her lack of self-control to touch the spinning wheel. How do we refrain from approaching those things that are enticing, or are habitual, or of a generational curse and cause us to walk right into the enemy's trap, keeping us under physical and spiritual strongholds?

Self-control shows up in various scenarios. We often refer to practicing self-control when it involves food, sex and behavior. Depending on how we manage these areas of our lives determines the paths we can end up on. We have free will in the choices we make in life. We can choose to eat healthy or not, to wait until marriage to have sex or or choose to pursue various sexual partners and we can choose how we react and behave in certain situations. Very often it is our freewill that entitles us to think we can do anything we want whenever we want, which is very true. It is, however, the consequences of when we neglect to make the right choice and practice self-control that should concern us. The Bible teaches us that just because we can do a thing does not mean we have to. In 1 Corinthians 10:23-24 we read, "You say, "I am allowed to do anything" – but not everything is good for you. You say, "I am allowed to do anything" – but not everything is beneficial. Don't be concerned for your own good but for the good of others." Yes, we can eat anything we want, but do our poor choices in food conflict with leading a healthy lifestyle before our children? Yes, we can give in to our sexual desires, however, outside of the potential exposure to diseases, we also expose ourselves to emotional and spiritual trauma. Additionally, how would our choice affect that sexual partner's faith walk? We may not realize this but they were probably relying on us to witness to them and hold them accountable. Yes, we can engage in extra-marital sex whenever we want, but what effect would that affair have on the survival of our marriage? Yes, we can 'clap-back' or curse out our spouses, co-workers, friends, or stranger, but does vulgar, unkind and random outbursts lend to further damaging a situation or relationship?

David had several opportunities to 'exercise his free will' and kill his greatest adversary, King Saul. He knew what he was capable of doing and had the opportunities to do it, but he didn't. Although coaxed by his team to kill the King, David chose to exercise self-control. He even proved this to the King by cutting a piece of King Saul's robe to show him he could have destroyed him, but he didn't. In showing the King this, the King was grateful for David's kindness. David recognized that this was not a fight he had to participate in. Even though he had the upper hand and was pretty much justified in attacking the King, he chose not to. He left the fate of King Saul to God.

Sometimes we are asked to be a part of things that we do not endorse, believe in or that is contrary to our values. Our spirits may be convicted with the things we do, the things we say or the thoughts we think. We may be convicted by the shows we watch, the music we listen to or the relationships we're in. We may encounter peer pressures or be tempted during our walk. It is our convictions that guide us when we are faced with submitting to the pressures and our flesh, but we choose to exercise self-control and hand the situation over to God. The three Hebrew boys allowed God to have complete control of the situation they found themselves in. We find that the three Hebrew boys discovered their self-control came from their confidence in God. They didn't fight the King, but stood by what they believed in and not wavering and accepted whatever may come their way when they declared: "But even if he doesn't, we want to make it clear to you, Your Majesty, that we will never serve your gods or worship the gold statue you have set up." (Daniel 3:18) What a stand to take! Think of the areas we lack self-control and idolize and how we could make this same declaration to honour our faith, our values and ourselves.

In contrast, we read about Peter who lacked self-control when Jesus was approached by a crowd led by Judas. When they were about to arrest and take Jesus, Peter cut off one of the high priest's slave's ear. Built up anger, snap reactions and defensive responses all show how lack of self-control can lead to potentially serious consequences. When we read this, it isn't uncommon to feel ashamed if we see ourselves in Peter when we think about how that last argument started or why we no longer speak to people or are disobedient to the word. But Jesus in all his compassion and grace, still finds time to teach through what was a moment of chaos. He repairs the man's ear, he heals him and rebukes Peter's behavior. He openly shows compassion and acts as a wise counsel to Peter.

And this applies to our lives as well. While we are pushing through and working on our self-control, during those times when we often slip up, let's not be discouraged, for the grace of God will repair that situation and heal that hurt. He will use our past to push us into our purpose. It is, however, when we avail ourselves to the discipline of self-control, that we bear witness to the positive life-changing results that follow. Jesus Christ himself had all the power in the world to come down from the Cross, but he even had to exercise self-control and undergo the greatest sacrifice out of love, offering salvation to those who choose it. Repeating his words daily will assist in practicing self-control "…I want your will to be done, not mine"(Luke 22:42).

HERE TO
SERVE YOU

CHAPTER 11

Proverbs 31:20

"She extends a helping hand to the poor
and opens her arms to the needy."

I AM...
HERE TO SERVE YOU

Mahatma Gandhi said, "The best way to find yourself is to lose yourself in the service of others." When I connected with the Rotarians over twenty years ago via the Rotary Exchange Student program where I traveled and lived in Mexico for just under one year, I learned they embodied the sentiments of Gandhi. During that time, I learned of their motto: *Service Above Self.* They understood that our time away from family for so long with little communication would be difficult, but serving and thinking of others would enable us to learn who we were and what we were capable of achieving.

It can be very easy to focus on our struggles, inconveniences or hardships, making them our primary focus especially when it seems like we are going through them every day. We go to sleep with the stresses of our day on our mind. Sometimes they keep us awake at night and our spirits are unsettled. We can become so caught up in this routine that it is easy to forget those things we are blessed with. We tend to have blinders on preventing us from seeing that there are also others around us suffering, sick, depressed, lost and who need the gifts God has given us to bless them. When we focus on our struggles and inconveniences, putting them over our call to serve, we miss out on discovering who we can truly be, failing to take a step closer toward our purpose.

With the calamities that happen around the world it is arrogant and naïve for us to think we are exempt from finding ourselves in a state of need. It is normal to empathize, but if we haven't been through the experience we could never truly imagine ourselves in such a horrible state. In contrast, many of us dwell in our needy state exchanging and comparing sob stories, throwing pity parties every chance we get. Neither one of these behaviors helps anybody, especially not ourselves.

Jesus came to serve not to be glorified and we are to follow in His ways. The parable of the Good Samaritan encourages us to serve and care for our neighbors (the second greatest commandment) and it clarifies who are neighbor is. During those times we allow our circumstances, positions and the obstacles in our life to consume us we overlook and forget about those who are right in front of us standing in need. You see, the priest and Temple assistant were too busy, too consumed with life or their circumstances or their position and missed the opportunity to bless the Jewish man who was attacked, robbed, injured and left for dead on the side of the road. They were probably rushing to a meeting or a class or had their minds occupied by something that stressed them out that day. They were so caught up in what was going on in their lives that they didn't even notice the man in his struggles. They were probably in a hurry to tell someone of what happened to them that they didn't even have the time to check on the man to see whether he needed to be helped. Or maybe in all their health, wealth and comfort, it was beneath them to get a little dirty to bend down to this man to listen to his pain or even pray for him. The story tells us the priest, "saw the man lying there and he crossed to the other side of the road and passed him by." He made a conscious effort to avoid any encounter with this man, maybe out of fear, maybe out of selfishness, or maybe by casting judgment. We are quick to pass the homeless everyday not even understanding why they are in that position, and like the priest, we consciously cross the road. Or maybe we are like the Temple assistant who did go to look at the man because he saw something was wrong but probably assumed that while the man was down he was not completely out; so it wasn't really his concern. He was breathing so that was enough reassurance for him that the man would make it and be okay.

How many people have we passed with a hello and a smile not even noticing that they were spiritually beaten and bruised, financially struggling, not knowing where their next meal would come from, or that their child was struggling and on drugs and becoming abusive, or they just suffered a miscarriage, trying to save their marriage or received a terminal diagnosis? Are we self-consumed that we overlook the concerns of our neighbors, our brothers and sisters, our strangers? Paul puts it bluntly in Galatians 6:2-3, "Share each other's burdens, and in this way obey the law of Christ. If you think you are too important to help someone, you are only fooling yourself. You are not that important."

Thinking back to the Rotarians' motto: *Service above self*, service can be as large or as small as you make it, but it begins with an encounter and with a soul of compassion. What is important is that what you do has a positive impact in someone's life, and because of their encounter with you, their life has been blessed no matter how big or small the deed. At the end of the parable it was the unlikely character, the Samaritan, who stopped to help the beaten and bruised Jewish man. He cleaned him up, put him on his donkey and took him to a nearby inn paying for his stay. The Bible tells us he had compassion for this man and purposely highlights the unlikely character as the one to show that compassion to bring home the point that no matter our differences, our comfort levels or circumstances, it should be the compassion within us, the love for God and His people, that moves us to care for one another. The Samaritan also recognized that God had blessed him to be a blessing to someone else. He was in good health to forgo his donkey, he had the skillset to take care of him and had means to put the man up in the inn for as long as it took. This alone should ignite a passion within you to think of how your gifts and blessings could bless your neighbor. God will never forget your sorrows, and just as He sends someone to serve you in your time of need, He wants you to serve others in their time of need. Remember these words, "I tell you the truth, when you did it to one of the least of these my brothers and sisters, you were doing it to me," and "I tell you the truth, when you refused to help the least of these my brothers and sisters, you were refusing to help me."

A WARRIOR NOT
A WORRIER

CHAPTER 12

Proverbs 31:21

"She has no fear of winter for her household, for everyone has warm clothes."

I AM...
A WARRIOR NOT A WORRIER

Living on an island in the middle of the Atlantic Ocean, I can tell you that almost yearly we are faced with the threat of a hurricane that can range between a Category 1 to 5. Several hurricanes have made landfall causing much destruction, but we have also been blessed to have many misses. Unlike our neighbors in the United States, we have to ride out each storm as it comes because we have no evacuation plans to accommodate relocating the 60,000 plus residents off the island. In recognizing this, our forefathers built homes and buildings that would withstand a minimum 110-mile per hour sustained winds. Their wisdom resulted in the very strict building codes that are currently in place. When building a home, we are required to build a solid foundation, the load bearing walls must use eight-inch concrete blocks and the roofs are made with slate or SKB that are able to bear a minimum load of fifty pounds. As you can imagine the process is long and expensive, but also necessary and invaluable.

When a hurricane becomes a threat, we are ordered to board up our windows and glass doors, stock up on canned goods, water and ice, have sufficient batteries, flashlights, and candles. As you can imagine, going through a storm is a very stressful and scary experience, however, the stress level depends on the strength of the storm. The preparation involved in building our homes gives a sense of comfort and peace to the residents who have experienced many hurricanes. We know that anything under a strong Category 3 has a lesser potential to cause great structural damage. We are cautious but not worried. Even when a great hurricane hits the island, while there will be structural damage and the winds are high and very scary, we are stressed and frightened for several hours, yet we are also ironically very confident that we will not receive mass destruction of infrastructure or flattened or uprooted homes. That confidence stems from our preparations, strict building codes and the strong foundation of our homes. This confidence led social media to coin the phrase #bermudastrong.

The parable of the house built on sand, compared to the house built on solid rock, is a basic yet very profound message that has some semblance to my #bermudastrong story. We learn about handling life's challenges based on how we have laid our spiritual foundation. Our spiritual and personal storms also range from a Category 1 to 5. We are comfortable with the mild storms and find it very easy to rely on our faith when we miss a flight, go through a cold or mild illness. Then a slightly stronger storm comes our way and the foundation of our faith is tested when we find ourselves saved and single at an age when everyone else is married with children or when we fail an exam or lose a job. But these storms do not break us as we rely on the hope that God has a better plan for us. But when that Category 4 or 5 storm stirs up, forecasted to make a direct hit on us, and finally making landfall, we start to witness the strength of our foundation. We start to see whether we have kept up the required maintenance to determine if we will crumble or withstand the high winds. These storms can include difficulty in our marriages, unexpected death, a critical diagnosis, financial crisis or natural disaster. A weak foundation can lead to divorce, depression, loss of self-control, abnormal behavior, self-destruction and giving up.

Like a physical structure, maintenance is critical to our spiritual structure. It takes a daily spiritual renewing. A renewing of the mind and daily creating a clean heart. Our foundation is reading the word of God, prayer and thanksgiving.

Reading the word: "But if you remain in me and my words remain in you, you may ask for anything you want, and it will be granted! When you produce much fruit, you are my true disciples. This brings great glory to my Father." (John 15:7-8)

Prayer and thanksgiving: "Don't worry about anything, instead, pray about everything. Tell God what you need and thank him for all he has done." (Philippians 4:6)

God tells us that life will have its challenges and He is concerned about the foundation we lay. He said the weapons will come against us, but they will not prosper. He said He will be with us through deep water, rivers of difficulty and fires of oppression. He wants us to give our burdens to Him so he can take care of us. When the storms come, and we feel like we are spinning out of control, it is the foundation that will remain and will prevent complete destruction.

Throughout the Bible we are constantly reminded of the kind of God we serve. The one who was there for Abraham, Isaac and Jacob. God wants us to anchor our hope in Him and remember He was there for them and He will be there for us. We can also look at our own lives. How could the God that brought your husband to you that you once loved dearly not also be the God that can fix your marital problems? How could the God who blessed you with this child not also be the God that can turn their life around? How could the God that delivered you from that last hurdle or burden many years ago not do the same for you or your loved ones today? How could the God whose son Jesus was tempted for forty days by Satan not provide you with a way out of temptation? And how could the God who sent His own son to die on the cross not understand your grief? It was He who sent the Holy Spirit as the Comforter.

God sent us many comforting promises to overcome worry. When we fill our hearts with these promises, we are laying that sturdy foundation for the storms that will come. When we are prepared and the foundation is laid, we may experience fear and concern, but can remain confident that we will not experience complete destruction. We can recognize the enemy for who he is, in his various forms and from the various angles he will try to come for us. Jesus did this with Judas when He saw the enemy in him. He told the enemy to do what he had to do so Jesus could do what He had to do! He was prepared for what was to come and confident with His preparation for what the outcome would be.

In Matthew 6:25-34 Jesus teaches us about overcoming worry. We learn to not worry about the little things in life as life is more than what we are currently going through. It is about the grace we will experience, the salvation we received, the daily blessings and sharing it all with others. It is about the choices we make to secure our eternal life.

Worrying will not solve any problem in our life. The question Jesus poses to us is the same question we should pose to ourselves: "Can all your worries add a single moment to your life?" If you are going through something that is causing you to worry and stress, ask yourself that question. If your answer is 'no' then I encourage you to hand it over to God, lay your burden at the altar. God wants to carry your load.

BECOMING A
BETTER ME

CHAPTER 13

Proverbs 31:22

"She makes her own bedspreads. She dresses
in fine linen and purple gowns."

I AM...
BECOMING A BETTER ME

When I read this verse I really started to think 'Is there anything this woman can't do?' She is a business woman, manages her household, revered by many and looks amazing while doing it. She seems to be committed to staying relevant and always evolving. She's committed to becoming better even when she's already great at what she does. There are no limits with her. She is a reminder to us that God has already provided us with everything we need to be all we were created to be.

We all have areas in our lives where we can do better, serve better, think better, love better and forgive better. I liken it to the SWOT analysis we undergo in the workplace when the Strengths, Weaknesses, Opportunities and Threats of the company are analysed to assess the viability of the company. Our personal SWOT analysis will identify our Strengths that distinguish us from others, that make us unique and when utilized, help strengthen the kingdom of God. The Weaknesses are those things that need identifying in order to be removed from our lives or that are blocking us from pursuing our purpose. We look for Opportunities where our Strengths can be used to improve our lives and the lives of others. Identifying the Threats our weaknesses could have on our lives, that if not addressed, will keep us from becoming our best self, involves checking attitudes, our outlook on life and how we overthink situations. We can assess our roles as a daughter, a wife, a friend, a colleague and a leader. Mostly we can assess our Christian walk and live what we believe through prayer, reading the Bible and discipleship. For me I had to study the Bible more to be equipped with Godly knowledge and not the knowledge of man. We may not get this right all the time and will struggle from time to time, but obtaining the experience and life lessons along the way are incomparable and extremely valuable.

There are times when we feel stuck in life or have lost our connection to God, and we find ourselves doubting Him. There are times we can't accept that our lives will get any better or be anything more than where we currently are. We may have given up for despair, lack of sight or experiencing immediate change. It is during these times that we must remember that God's great power is released in our great faith. We see how, in Luke 1, Zechariah's lack of faith limited God's fullness in his life. His mouth was shut when he didn't believe his elderly wife Elizabeth would give birth to their son, John. Imagine the things that have been shut out of our lives due to doubting that God's power could extend beyond our carnal knowledge, resulting in missed opportunities or not experiencing full joy.

In Mark 6:5-6, Jesus was disappointed with the lack of faith his own people had against him. He wanted to do so much more for them, but "because of their unbelief, he couldn't do any miracles among them except to place his hands on a few sick people and heal them. And he was amazed at their unbelief." In both of these passages, we see God's blessings flowing, but what we also see the fullness of God's power limited. The fullness of our potential and purpose is limited. The fullness of repaired relationships is blocked, the release of strongholds is withheld, financial freedom is delayed. We have to believe that we can be better than where we currently are, whatever that may look like. That we will think differently, that we will act differently and speak differently. That we will not complain, that our circumstances will not define us, that the need for validation will not move us, that we will be the light in dark times and the salt of the earth.

We are the only ones who can make the necessary changes and choices needed to better ourselves. We will declare those things in our life that we want and that we are. We will make these daily declarations. We will be uncomfortable at first, but these unfamiliar waters are necessary in the journey and the more we declare, the more confident we will be. Declare your "I am..." today!

MINDFUL OF
MY COMPANY

CHAPTER 14

Proverbs 31:23

"Her husband is well known at the city gates, where he sits with the other civic leaders."

I AM...
MINDFUL OF MY COMPANY

We live during a time where our lives are on display for the world to see. We make it a point that we are seen by others as being important. We make a point to have friends and strangers who will think our lives are exciting, that the people we know are exciting and the more people see us, the more popular we will be.

Proverbs 31:23 gives some insight to the kind of man this woman attracted and married. He is prominent, an upstanding citizen, well respected and is connected to other influential people as he holds a noble position in his community. Here we learn that we will associate with many people, but there should be people who are close to us that we learn from and hold up in higher regard, respect and honour. Ideally, we should surround ourselves with not only successful, happy and secure people, but we should also surround ourselves with those who hold us accountable. When it comes to matters of the heart, it's okay to live in a bubble. A friend of mine attended a school known for producing amazing singers and musicians. It was part of their curriculum and overall culture. He told me an interesting story about how he always knew how to sing. Everyone in his family, in his school and in his church, could sing very well. He never knew that people could not actually sing until he stepped outside of that environment.

The message was profound and made me reflect about my immediate circle and surroundings. If you make a conscious (or even subconscious) effort to surround yourself with successful, positive, supportive, uplifting people, who embrace happiness, peace and love, you wouldn't be accustomed to what the opposite looks like and that behavior will become foreign to you. When the behavior is foreign it will speak to your soul telling it that this is not a part of who you are and you will be less inclined to gravitate toward it. It doesn't mean you will be exempt from being in the presence of it, but your spirit will know better than to take it on.

Let us examine our surroundings. What are we known for in our circle of friends or in our community? And equally, how does this apply to those we associate with or call our friends? The kind one or the angry one? The reasonable one or the petty one? The joker or very serious one? The praying one or complaining one? The encourager or discourager? Optimist or pessimist? Where do you stand and where do those in your circle stand? We are familiar with the saying from childhood 'show me your friends and I'll show you who you are.' Of course, I never believed this until I started to see the different affects certain people would have in my life. It was a very difficult revelation to learn that going through seasons was both environmental and spiritual. I soon accepted that just like our natural surroundings it was spiritually necessary for change to happen. I traversed through the bitter coldness of life finding myself being surrounded by negativity, gossiping and unkindness that naturally influenced my character and I, too, became that person. I was bitter about situations in my life that I could not control but allowed them to control me. The warmth of the fiery tongues I once laughed at soon turned on me burning me badly.

Recognising this could no longer be the norm in my life, I relied on prayer and fasting and slowly began to see things begin to shed allowing the God in me to bloom. The law of attraction became very important to me. I wanted what was drawn to me to be a reflection of what I was putting out into the world. Of course, I'm still a work in progress in this area, but the key word is 'work' and working on this daily has yielded great returns. Once I opened myself up to more positive energy, I allowed myself to encounter amazing and empowering people and positive energy entered into my space and I was exposed to unbe-lievable opportunities.

Rather than being seen as important, be important. Become a change agent in your community. Find positive mentors and role models to emulate. Find your Ruth who will nurture you through the uncertainties of life. Find your Samuel who will hold you accountable when you are wrong and will guide you back when you stray. Find your Elizabeth who will awaken that passion inside of you and help you to birth your vision and dreams. Find your Titus 2 mentor - the one who gives you godly wisdom and direction. These people will help guide you toward a successful life, whatever that looks like to you. Your success can be found finan-cially, through a peaceful and happy life, through spiritual connection or a worry-free mind. Define your success and then seek those who will help you obtain it.

Proverbs 27:17 "Iron sharpens iron so a friend sharpens a friend."

MORE THAN A
CONQUEROR

CHAPTER 15

Proverbs 31:24

**"She makes belted linen garments and
sashes to sell to the merchants."**

I AM...
MORE THAN A CONQUEROR

Dress has always been important throughout the centuries of time. It was one identifiable way to distinguish wealth, status and family lineage. Understanding the importance of clothing, it is no surprise that the Proverbs 31 woman served a need of the people, providing them with fine garments and sashes for their daily wear. Fashion is ever evolving and is influenced by culture, music and environment. Even today, looking at how one dresses, you can make an assumption about their lifestyle, wealth and status. Also, one's livelihood dictates how one presents themselves, which can be entirely different from how they would dress for a special occasion, church or formal event. We understand that some attire is appropriate in one setting while inappropriate in another.

As women, we often struggle with the 'nothing to wear' syndrome when looking into a closet full of clothes and shoes. Going out on a date or meeting up with the girls can turn an immaculate bedroom into a war zone within a span of one or two hours. The decision can be most difficult! We tend to have our favorite outfits to impress, to feel empowered and to feel sexy. We hope if we look a certain way we can feel a certain way and people can perceive us in a certain way. It is, however, the spiritual dress that gives us that inner empowerment and peace that exudes on the outside and makes the most impact no matter how we are outwardly dressed. When people need real people, they look beyond your outer appearance and are drawn to the spirit within you. Our spiritual dress is influenced by our habits, our daily practices and commitments. When dealing with minor spiritual battles or the extremes of life, it is our spiritual preparedness that will help us conquer the battles that will come our way.

In Ephesians 6, we are warned and informed about the daily battles and struggles we will encounter. I say 'warned' as that is God preparing us for what is to come, and I say 'informed' as that is God educating us about the attacks being spiritual attacks and not physical attacks, and how we are to prepare for them. And when we are prepared, we dwell in the presence and promises of God. Whatever battles come our way, it is our first reaction in the flesh to receive them personally. We look at the struggles, unexpected events and crises in our lives as a personal attack against us and our response becomes personal. When we remove the personal aspect, and understand that there is a spiritual battle happening around us, we can then learn to fight spiritually and not physically. Ephesians 6:11-19 warns us of the strategies of Satan who is constantly on the prowl seeking whom he can devour. We are enlightened to the fact that what is happening to us is beyond this physical realm. In order to conquer these moments in our life we must remain prepared.

In the last few years, it feels like I have heard conversations amongst groups of people expressing their confusion and frustration about the events that are happening around the world. Events and circumstances that tend to be beyond their control or becoming out of control. Events like hurricanes, floods, fires, civil wars, genocide, racial attacks, gang violence and unexpected deaths. Events like mental breakdowns, the breakdown of the community, the church and the family unit. These are the events that create shock within the community and we come together to think of solutions, yet we feel hopeless when all we have tried has failed. These are also the events that create anger, doubt and fear. These feelings arise when we lack understanding and are ill-prepared to fight in the spiritual realm. The same way we rummage through our closets for that perfect outfit is how we should rummage through our spiritual closets to suit up for our daily battles.

The warning: Ephesians 6:11, "...stand firm against all strategies of the devil." The Bible warns us many times of the attacks of the enemy. They will come in many forms, from many angles and both internally and externally. We are warned about the sole purpose of Satan to kill, steal and destroy. To kill our hope, steal our joy and destroy our minds and lives.

The information: Ephesians 6: 12, "For we are not fighting against flesh and blood enemies, but against evil rulers and authorities of the unseen world, against mighty powers in this dark world, and against evil spirits in the heavenly places." When we are informed we can make informed decisions based on truth rather than hypotheticals or misunderstanding. Our reactions and responses are then based on compassion and love.

The preparation: Ephesians 6:13-19, "Therefore, put on every piece of God's armor so you will be able to resist the enemy in the time of evil." This consists of:

Belt of Truth, Body armor of Righteousness, Shoes of Peace, Shield of Faith, Helmet of Salvation, Sword of the Spirit which is the word of God. Being warned and properly informed assists with adequate preparation. We can prepare our hearts and minds to shift focus from the person, our personal desires or situation and address the spiritual forces around us.

The promise: Ephesians 6:13(b), "Then after the battle you will still be standing firm." In order to conquer anything and overcome situations and be declared a winner or champion or survivor we will have to go through some things, but "despite all these things, overwhelming victory is ours through Christ, who loved us" (Romans 8:27 NLT) or "...we are more than conquerors through him that loved us" (KJV).

Yes, we will have struggles, heartache, unexpected battles, trauma and tragedy, but remain steadfast in knowing we will overcome and will be conquerors. We can do all things through Christ who strengthens us. We can overcome our past, choose a more positive solution, pray, fast and believe God will turn any situation around. We are better than what tries to keep us down. Whatever was meant for evil WILL be turned for your good. We are more than conquerors!

WEARING
MY CROWN

CHAPTER 16

Proverbs 31:25

"She is clothed with strength and dignity, and she laughs without fear of the future."

I AM...
WEARING MY CROWN

In Chapter 13 we dove into the physical presence of the Proverbs 31 woman. Here we will focus on the beauty that dwells from within her. Living during a time where many things compete for our attention, it is usually the loudest, the flashiest, and the negative that comes out on top for the win. Social media, television, music, and fashion all influence our lives. They are repeatedly referred to as the distractions of life. While there is truth behind this statement, the fact is that how these outlets influence you is solely your responsibility.

The second greatest commandment in the Bible is: "You shall love your neighbor as yourself." (Mark 12:31) Simply put, we have to be in a right position spiritually and emotionally in order to be our most authentic selves to others. Our authenticity includes setting boundaries on how we are treated, on how our time and feelings are respected and how we respect ourselves.

Without a doubt it is a wonderful time to be alive. Technology and science have proven to enhance our lives at exceptional rates. Information is received at the speed of light and over-sharing information, well, is delivered even faster. It can be difficult to balance the beneficial use of these enhancements to our lives with the detrimental effects they could have. Many of us have been caught up in our social media use. Our insecurities are targeted more and more as is seen in highly controversial photo-shopped pictures, the denigration of women in music lyrics, videos and movies and the high ratings of drama-filled 'reality' shows that feature housewives that aren't wives of any-one, and that exploit our sexuality and encourage vulgar behavior, promiscuity and adultery. These representations of us as women are being dictated to us in overt and co-vert ways. And when we are not alert to their effects we don't even recognize our behavior slowly reflecting what we see and absorb. So, exposing our sexuality is confused as "freedom of expression." Using derogatory words to describe ourselves and other females is confused as "empow-ering," emancipating ourselves from the need of a man and emasculating them at the same time is confused as being an "independent woman." The pattern here is that our state of confusion leads to accepting otherwise abnormal behavior as normal behavior.

Daily our identity is being challenged. We must ask ourselves, "What will we answer to?" and "What will we allow to define us?" No matter where we are in this conun-drum, we have hope that it is never too late to redefine who we are. We may have messed up in the past whether publicly or privately which brings us shame, but it is our decision on how we allow that to define us and shape our lives that matters. It matters to God and it should matter to us. Knowing our insecurities and inhibitions are being tested is key to circumventing the tactics set out to destroy us and to refocus on loving and respecting ourselves more.

The enemy knows where your weaknesses lie and will try everything to cause you to think you are unworthy, inadequate, worth of nothing more than your sexuality and physical appearance. Remember, Satan tried this with Jesus. He tried to play on the human insecurities of greed, power and physical needs. Jesus, however, had his security placed in the hand of God. He knew that nothing Satan offered could surpass anything His Father already had. Jesus had been through this battle and He is the example that we remain strong when we remain connected to the vine (John 15:5). As long as we are in the world we are the light of the world (John 9:5).

The Samaritan woman at the well in John 4 had five husbands (not necessarily hers). She was defined by her act of adultery. In fact, it was how Jesus had identified her, not to shame her but to offer her deliverance and for her to choose that day what she would answer to in the future. We read of another adulterer in the Bible who was also known by her sin that pushed the town to have her stoned. But it was Jesus who reminded the people of the town that none of us are without sin and that we can be redeemed from whatever state we are in. We can push past that which has kept us in bondage and choose to see ourselves and love ourselves as God does. That is called standing tall, with our heads high, releasing all shame and guilt. When we do that, we are wearing our crowns. It is our choice. Do we allow the drama, the bad relationship, the gossip, our manipulation and jealousy to define us? Do we allow our jobs, our state of mind, our sickness, our children or our homes to define us? How do you see yourself and how do you love yourself? This brings me to the expectations we allow others to have on us. How we allow people to respect our time and the expectations we set.

We talked about the 'superwoman' syndrome earlier in this book, which largely stems from the expectations we give to others that are later taken for granted. At work we put in extended hours that keep us away from home and if we are home we are still working either via our cellphones or laptops. We don't disconnect and create balance in our lives. Then in our homes we are burdened with many tasks that we insist on taking on ourselves partly because we don't trust others (spouse, parents, children, family) to do them. We somehow convince ourselves that this is how it has to be and ultimately, we experience burnout. We find ourselves yielding to the needs of others and doing for everyone and when it's our turn to be supported we find ourselves disappointed when those people do not show up.

I have found that we like to say we are busy. That we are busy with church and work, busy running the kids around, that we are overwhelmed, that we work crazy hours. Subconsciously we tend to involve ourselves in stuff and things leaving little time to really self-reflect and create boundaries to allow that quiet time with ourselves and with God. We tend to forget how to use that little word 'no.' Mary saw the importance of setting boundaries and expectations and using that time to spend with her Savior and learn at his very feet. She did not allow Martha's expectations of her to dictate how she should feel and how she should be in this certain situation. She understood the importance of and respected herself enough to have her "me time." She did not allow Martha's frustration, manipulation and victimization to discourage or deflate her and have her give in to something that she did not want to do. She put first what she valued the most. The Bible never mentions Mary saying anything in response to Martha's tyrants. But her posture surely said enough.

We owe it to ourselves to speak up and defend ourselves. We do this from a point of love, a point of respect and honesty. Each time we allow our boundaries to be broken or allow ourselves to be attacked, manipulated, or disregarded we start to lower our shoulders, lower our eyes, lower our heads and our crown starts to slip off. As women we battle with a lot both internally and externally. We constantly deal with setting boundaries and balance in our lives and learning what is acceptable behavior and unacceptable behavior. It's time to love us again. We can only give of ourselves what we ourselves have. The Message Bible translates the very familiar verse Psalm 23:5 in this way: "You revive my drooping head (that's God lifting your head so you can fix your crown); my cup brims with blessing (that's God allowing you to be full again and the overflow is to bless others)."

SPEAKING
LIFE

CHAPTER 17

Proverbs 31:26

"When she speaks, her words are wise, and she gives instructions with kindness."

I AM...
SPEAKING LIFE

Most churches within the African Methodist Episcopal Church recite the Call to Worship every Sunday. Within that there is the Bible verse from Psalm 19:14, "May the words of my mouth and the meditation of my heart be acceptable in your sight, oh Lord my strength and my redeemer." We recite this so often that it is easy for its meaning and effect to be lost. Scripture teaches us numerous ways in which our words are important in the way they affect us and others.

We often think the purpose of communication is to exchange information, but what life teaches us is that we really communicate to be heard and to be understood. Communicating to be heard and understood are to ensure our survival. We learn this with the first breath we take into this world. We don't know how to speak or understand the art of communication, but the doctor spanks our bottoms to hear our screams and gauge our healthiness to ensure our survival. Our screams communicate to the doctor that we are breathing strong and are ready to begin our lives. Exchanging information is important, but when it comes to entering into meaningful relationships, under-standing that both parties are communicating to be heard is integral to the survival of that relationship. Keeping this in mind will help shape your conversations and create ef-fective communication with one another. So therefore, communication involves listening to what is being said and responding accordingly and not responding just to get your point across.

Our communication starts within the mind and heart, that which we meditate on, the things we dwell on or the scenarios we create in our minds. It's what we meditate on that is eventually revealed in our words. Thinking about the 'dreaded' upcoming Monday after a good weekend is reflected with the "I hate Mondays" phrase and normally results in regretting having to go to work and not having a progressive day or not appreciating the job. How about when our minds wonder after reading a misinterpreted text message? We create all sorts of scenarios and drama in our heads that tend to play out in real life. When we dwell on something that has bothered us for some time with our jobs or relationship, it is reflected in our attitude and in the tone of our voices. How we think about ourselves and others, whether negatively or positively, becomes evident in our interactions with others. Perfecting this internal communication is integral to the survival of our sanity. The most important conversations you have on a daily basis are with God and yourself. Mastering these daily communica-tions will set the foundation for effective communication with your loved ones and peers.

What we communicate to ourselves shapes and guides what we think of ourselves, how we treat ourselves and what we think of others and how we treat others. Paul describes this in Philippians 4:8, "And now, dear brothers and sisters, one final thing. Fix your thoughts on what is true, and honourable, and right, and pure and lovely, and admirable. Think about things that are excellent and worthy of praise." Meditating on these things will be the difference needed so our words create life and not bring death to situations, the difference needed so our words do not condemn us but acquit us and the difference needed to uplift others and not bring them down. Often, this will require us to make a conscious effort to pause before speaking to allow us to check our thoughts and how they will reflect through our words.

This leads us to the next key ingredient to communicating which is listening. Actively listening shows that you care about what the person is saying and you have set that time for only them. Those moments spent listening are without interruption, without cellphones, or any other distractions. A listening ear is what many people want. Remember we communicate to be heard and understood. You can see the frustration in people when they feel as if they have not been heard. You yourself know what this feels like. I remember my godson took a while to develop adequate communication skills. He did not properly form words until he was almost five; so people constantly had to ask him to repeat what he was saying. He had a lot to say; but, when he had to constantly repeat himself he became frustrated and frustration led to anger. If you did not know him you would think he had anger problems, but he had communication and lack of being understood problems. Many of us are in a similar state. We have communication and lack of being understood problems that lead us to frustration and anger. We have misunderstandings, outbursts, lies and manipulation problems that break up friendships, families and marriages. They create animosity, spite, the silent treatment and unnecessary jealousy. All of this because of a negative mindset, lack of listening leading to failed communication. One of my favorite quotes on this topic is in the acronym T.H.I.N.K.

Is it **T**rue?
Is it **H**elpful?
Is it **I**nspiring?
Is it **N**ecessary?
Is it **K**ind ?

Let's THINK about the impact of our words.
Let's THINK about the importance of our words.
Let's THINK about the change that can happen with our words.

CHERISHING
WHAT I VALUE

CHAPTER 18

Proverbs 31:27

"She carefully watches everything in her household and suffers nothing from laziness."

I AM...
CHERISHING WHAT I VALUE

Value can be measured in various ways. It can be measured with our commitment, the time we spend, the money we spend, our sacrifice or the way we treat things and people. We tend to place more value in one thing over another and this can fluctuate depending on the circumstances of our lives. In my younger years I used to value having friends and now I value having loyalty. I used to value my position within the church and now I value my witness to God's people. I used to value the ladies' man and now I value the man of God. I used to value my career advancement and now I value my purpose in life. The more time passes, the more you experience in life, the more you become aware of how you value time, loved ones and peace of mind.

In this particular verse the woman tirelessly watches over everything in her household. The household or the home is our most sacred place. It is where we are most comfortable and familiar. It's where the people closest to us see the best and worst of us. It is the place where many secrets are held. It is the place where we are glad the four walls can't talk. It is in the home that we are most challenged to be the best witnesses for God for it is where our character and faith are frequently tested and shaken, but also strengthened. It is where we set our core values. Remember we spoke of women being the foundation of their community and household. She does this by ensuring the home is not compromised as she tirelessly watches over everything. She ensures her family is cared for, loved and prayed over. These are the non-materialistic things that make up our core values. The love, concern, respect and prayer life we tirelessly protect, put ahead of everything else and uphold everyday.

I liken these core values to the Fruits of the Spirit. If you have not set core values for your life, Galatians 5:22-23 can be your starting point. The nine fruits of the spirit: love, joy, peace, patience, kindness, goodness, faithfulness, gentleness and self-control are basic principles to help formulate your core values. They are pretty basic yet somehow have become very complex in obtaining and maintaining. Your core values may include time management, morals, faith, communication and family. To maintain peace, love and self-control, we manage our time. We limit our frustration and anger by being mindful of whom we spend our time with and what we spend our time doing, thereby limiting wasted time. Also spending quality time and being considerate of other people's time is a form of love and respect. Adhering to our morals and upholding our faith attracts goodness and kindness to our lives and establishes boundaries. Our morals and faith will be tested and it's our love, patience, kindness and faithfulness that direct how we handle ourselves. We learn to exercise self-control in antagonizing situations and will be seen as the peacemaker and respected as a leader. It is also an opportunity to demonstrate our faithfulness to God and to our convictions. When we are committed to having positive, effective communication, our words are gentle and kind and bring peace, love, and joy.

Finally, we maintain the family unit by upholding each one of the nine fruits of the spirit. When uncompromised and honoured, the family respects one another, upholds one another, protects one another, forgives one another, supports one another, communicates with one another and most of all shows unconditional love toward one another.

Core values guide you through the course of your lifetime and direct your behavior, surroundings and intimate moments. They are something that you are willing to fight for and the things that you cherish in life outside of material items. They define you. Defining them and living them can either make you or break you. One of John C. Maxwell quotes is: "Your core values are the deeply held beliefs that authentically describe your soul."

In Matthew 26 we come to a greater understanding of the importance of where our core values derive from. When an unknown woman (in Luke 7 she is described as an immoral woman) heard of Jesus' arrival she met Him bringing an alabaster jar filled with expensive perfume and poured it over His head. The disciples thought this was such a waste as the perfume could have been sold for a high price and the money could have been given to the poor. While they tried to disguise their concern of the wasted perfume as a thought towards the poor Jesus saw right through them. Luke 7 fleshes out how the disciples were more disgusted that Jesus would commune with such a woman. Jesus highlighted that this woman (immoral or otherwise) valued the time Jesus would be there in the flesh and how she may never have that quality time before Him again. She of course knew the high price value of the perfume, but that did not override how much she valued being in the presence of Jesus at that time and how she would worship and honour Him in her own way. He stressed to the disciples, "You will always have the poor among you, but you will not always have me" (Matthew 26:11). When we think about our core values let's think about those things that are so precious that no money or worldly concerns could replace their eternal impact on our lives.

THE CHANGE I
WANT TO SEE

CHAPTER 19

Proverbs 31:28

**"Her children stand and bless her.
Her husband praises her."**

I AM...
THE CHANGE I WANT TO SEE

Trailblazers never really set out to change the world. They are usually someone who was ambitious enough to press forward amidst difficulty. They are someone who had many failed attempts, but never gave up. Their tenacity and endurance is what led to their achievements and recognition as one who successfully made a necessary change in this world. We usually know about the success and admire the highlight reel of their life without fully understanding the hard work, struggles and disappointments they had to go through to get them to that point. Then we also have many unsung heroes that are amongst us everyday. The ones who move silently through life, blazing their own trails, handling multiple jobs to do the best for their families, those who advocate on behalf of the less fortunate and unheard, those who are creating a better life for themselves, those who go to spiritual battle on behalf of others by fasting and through intercessory prayer. Then there are those who are suffering silently but openly give from what's left of them, those who contemplate suicide but make the decision to live another day as they find meaning in their life and want to give hope to others. There are those who struggle with addictions and choose to seek help knowing there is a better way, or those who dedicate their time bringing out the best in others. We all have the potential to blaze our own trails in our own ways.

When we look at the story of Queen Esther, it is clear she did not realize the influence she would ultimately have in her community or that she would be called on as a change agent. Her start in life would have been a perfect excuse for her to end up on a trail that could have led her on a self-destructive path. She suffered a traumatic loss by losing both parents, being left orphaned and raised by her cousin, Mordecai. It was her cousin that believed in her and helped her recognize the power in her purpose. Like Esther, we can find ourselves either climbing the ladder of success or equally falling off it into despair for such a long time that we do not realize what is happening in the community and world around us. We essentially become disconnected. But thankfully every now and then we get that reminder that we can be the change that is needed to move things forward, to mend relationships or create opportunities. That reminder could be a call on your life that is recognized by others such as being the go to person to organize events, to help others, to pray or lead in certain areas. Or the reminder could be that tug on your soul pulling you to do something impactful or speak out against an injustice. Whatever it is, Mordecai states it perfectly to Queen Esther, "Who knows if perhaps you were made queen for just such a time as this?" (Esther 4:14) He was calling on Queen Esther to speak against the killing that was planned against the Jews. While she initially thought she lacked such power or influence, Mordecai reminded her of the impact her inactions would have on the Jews of which she was also one. When we neglect to obediently move on the calling on our life we have inadvertently neglected and disappointed many others who look up to us or rely on us or are coming up behind us. One of the greatest compliments I have received in life is when someone let's me know that something I said or did had a positive impact on their life. I am immediately reminded of William McDowell's words in his song "I give myself away" that says, 'My life is not my own, to you I belong, I give myself to you'.

We will experience and see many injustices in our lifetime. We will experience dismay in our communities and churches. We ourselves will go through extremely difficult and trying times, but our outlook, our attitude and responses to each of these situations can create the change we want to see. We have to look at our life as not our own, but belonging to God and to make a difference for others. We may be in a position of influence or may have experience with defeat, death or despair. Whatever state we are in, we must ask ourselves the question, "Have I been put in this situation or gone through this experience for such a time as this?" Such a time as to counsel someone else, to provide advice on how to navigate their difficult moment, to put in a good word to a person of influence on behalf of someone or to raise funds for a organization in need or bring awareness to an injustice, or to tutor young men and women. Overall am I here to be a change agent? And if so, I must own it and recognize I am here to be the change!

WALKING IN
GREATNESS

CHAPTER 20

Proverbs 31:29

"There are many virtuous and capable women
in the world, but you surpass them all!"

I AM...
WALKING IN GREATNESS

Throughout this book we have explored the many different facets that make up the Proverbs 31 woman, the virtuous woman that we may struggle to be all the time, yet we can rest assured that we possess her qualities at some time in our lives. No matter what stage we are in life - whether we are living successful happy lives, are on our way to discovering our purpose or just living in the moment, through the ups and downs, the twists and turns, we must always find the ability to encourage ourselves. We must be our greatest cheerleaders. Talk ourselves through those difficult, crazy moments. Have those "come to Jesus" talks with ourselves. Tell ourselves it's going to be okay. Be our own wise counsel and seek help when needed. We must not forget, however, that we are surrounded by other amazing, virtuous, capable women, who are experiencing similar situations, and we are not in this alone.

We understand and easily recognize when people prey on our weaknesses, aiming to bring us down resulting in our silence. We shrink when we should speak up and be bold. But it's when people prey on our strengths that things get more complicated: our confidence, our intelligence, our beauty, our love, our honesty, our faithfulness, our security, all that makes us strong through the eyes of others are attacked through manipulation, jealousy, hate, deceit, disingenuous behavior, bullying and all under the guise of loving or supportive words, information gathering or in the name of Jesus. We don't understand it. We don't know what it is we have done wrong. We run scenarios back through our minds and by friends to understand what we could have done differently. But nothing comes to mind. In some situations it is just who you are. Your destiny for greatness will not be understood by all. It was true for David, the shepherd boy who became a King.

From 1 Samuel chapter 18 to the end of that book, chapter 31, we learn of how David was constantly preyed on by King Saul simply because of the life God had predestined for him. David was a diligent worker and liked by many. King Saul recognized David's greatness yet became very jealous and intimidated by David's favour. David however, could not understand the King's persistence in destroying him for he did everything the King asked, even killed a giant for him! He ran the scenarios through his mind and by his friend, the King's son, Jonathan, and there was no solid explanation. What made it more complicated was that his attacks were not consistent. As the King did recognize David's greatness, he constantly blessed him, but his jealousy and insecurities took over him and caused him to seek out various opportunities to destroy David. Yet David in all of his wisdom respected this man, a man anointed by God, and never retaliated in the natural but operated in the supernatural. He sought out God and prayed and left the fate of King Saul up to God. David teaches us that we will be attacked, taken off course, but that should never change our ultimate destination; rather it should propel us toward a deeper compassion for others, changing the trajectory of our lives, and why we do what we do (and who we do it for).

The scripture 1 John 4:4, "Greater is He that is in you than he that is in the world," became my anchor to God that helped me to keep it together when things started to fall apart, or people were trying to pull me apart. This particular verse allowed me to remove myself from many situations and allowed me to see myself as less of a victim when I was being attacked or seeking less credit or attention when I had been successful. It allowed me to have greater compassion for others and to see them how God saw them. It allowed me to pray for them rather than fight against them. To many, greatness may be a lifestyle, but I believe greatness is a mindset. One does not have to live a lavish lifestyle to be great. With peace of mind and a spirit of gratitude, you will find yourself seeing life in its purest form and cultivate a life around you filled with truth, honesty and love.

When we recognize that the greatness within us is of God and not of this world we will stop misunderstanding love with lust or emotional abuse. Once we recognize that the greatness within us is of God and not of this world, we no longer have to prove people wrong, convince people of our abilities, respond to the manipulators or entertain the insecurities of others. Recognizing that what may have been perceived as threatening to others are actually God-given gifts and abilities, we can communicate there was no need for a threat, but rather an opportunity to receive love. We no longer have to fight these worldly battles. The problem someone has with you or the attack against you is really against God because all of you that is great is because of God.

God has already predestined you for greatness and it is His voice that we must hear above all others. The voice that tells us His plans for us are good, gives us a future and hope, not disaster (Jeremiah 29:11). The voice that tells us if we delight ourselves in Him, He will give us the desires of our hearts (Psalms 37:4). The voice that tells us He has blessed us with every spiritual blessing in the heavenly realm (Ephesians 1:3). The voice that tells us He will accomplish infinitely more than we might ask or think (Ephesians 3:20); For no eye has seen, no ear has heard, and no mind has imagined what God has prepared for those who love him (1 Corinthians 2:9).

THANKFUL!

CHAPTER 21

Proverbs 31:30

"Charm is deceptive, and beauty does
not last; but a woman who fears the
Lord will be greatly praised."

I AM...
THANKFUL!

The first and greatest commandment is, "You must love the Lord your God with all your heart, all your soul, and all your mind." Jesus makes this declaration in the Gospels of Matthew, Mark and Luke.

Throughout this book we have delved into the attributes, the tenacity, the strength and perseverance of the Proverbs 31 woman, but here we see how she recognizes that everything she is, all of her accomplishments, all of her regality means absolutely nothing without a relationship with God. She fears the Lord and understands His word, His discipline and His love. She values life and does not take any day for granted for she could be stripped of everything at the turn of any unforeseen event, and yet even if that should happen, she is assured she will always have God and He is always in control. The way she fears God is seen in the way she obeys, worships and respects God. Fear does not mean to be afraid; rather, fear is a form of respect and of love.

In our attempt to form romantic relationships, we make special efforts to spend time with this new man that has entered our lives. We understand that spending time with someone is really the only way you can come to know him. We learn more about their character, what makes them happy or what makes them tick. We learn their likes and dislikes, their idiosyncrasies and habits. We invest our time both physically and emotionally and expect the same to be reciprocated. Over time a level of dependency, trust and security develops. We know their voice, we know their walk and we even know their smell. This is a love affair developing. If we can easily develop this Eros love for man, who may or may not add meaning to our lives, why not develop an eternal love for our Heavenly Father who created us! The love our God wants reciprocated is in the ways we worship Him with our heart, soul and mind.

Love your God with…

All your heart:

The universal symbol for love is depicted by the heart. Hearts are displayed all over Valentine's cards or drawn on trees and in the sand when couples display their love for one another. The heart is where our emotions become stirred up so much so that there have been people who have experienced extreme sadness from the loss of a loved one and have literally died of a broken heart. The pull of the heart is so strong that God urges us to protect it. In Proverbs 4:23 it is written, "Guard your heart above all else, for it determines the course of your life."

We need to strengthen our spiritual hearts to protect us from making irrational, spiteful or damaging decisions because we don't understand the love God has for us. Guarding your heart will help control reacting to situations based on emotions. God is not a god who has emotional reactions, He is a God of love (which can include tough love). When our world turns upside down and we turn our backs on God, He does not turn His back on us. He understands those times when we are taken for a loop, experience disappointments or loss. It is during these times that He wants us to remember just how much He loved us that He sent His only son to die on the cross for us to save us, to deliver us, to comfort us, to protect us and to provide a way. Yes, He loved us with all of His heart.

God is always pursuing us. And the pursuit doesn't end when we find Him, the way it does in some of our worldly relationships. No, it's a constant pursuit. Psalm 23 gives a synopsis of some of the many ways God's love supersedes all we are and all we go through and it reminds us of God's goodness. We are reminded that He is concerned about the matters of the heart and His unfailing love pursues us all the days of our lives. As He pursues us He wants us to pursue Him. If we search for God wholeheartedly, we will find Him (Jeremiah 29:13). Let us remember when it comes to matters of the heart, "Love never gives up, never loses faith, is always hopeful, and endures through every circumstance." (1 Corinthians 13:7). Say it. Repeat it. Apply it.

All your soul:

The phrase 'soul ties' and 'soul mate' is loosely used and often misunderstood. When we come into an intimate relationship with a man we claim to form soul ties with that man. When I reconnected with a former boyfriend I swore down he was my soul mate. I quickly learned that this was not so. There was a spirit that was drawing me, and it was the spirit of infatuation, confusion and loneliness. When it comes to a true soul mate, to me it is he who speaks to our soul and it is our soul that speaks to him.

When God created us, it was His spirit that gave us life. "God breathed life into man and man became a living soul" (Genesis 2:7). Our souls are the spirit of God breathed into us and that dwells within us. It's the spirit of God that keeps us moving forward and gives us joy. When we love ourselves, we are loving God. When we love God, we are loving ourselves. Loving God with all your soul is going all in, without distraction, pride or judgment. It's worshipping God in truth and in spirit. The truth of the word lifts our spirits toward God. It is surrendering our all. It's being still in God's presence. It's tarrying in prayer for one more hour.

Now it's the Holy Spirit that has come to comfort us and guide us. It's the Holy Spirit that speaks on our behalf when we do not know what to say. It speaks to us or we like to call it our 'sub-conscious'. It's that little voice that we can ignore from time to time, but later regret not listening to it. It's our 'intuition', 'first mind' or 'gut feeling'. All of this is to say that when we love God with all our soul we are spending quality time with Him so we can know His voice, being transformed to be more like Him, examining ourselves within, possessing the fruits of the spirit and aligning the desires of our hearts with the desires God has planned for our life. It's allowing the Holy Spirit to come in and take precedence in our lives. "Since we are living by the Spirit, let us follow the Spirit's leading in every part of our lives" (Galatians 5:25). It's that love language like when you and your spouse can finish each other's sentences or can communicate with each other without saying anything. It's like the private jokes you share and the secrets you share with each other. When you have that soul tie with God, you can trust He holds the intimate parts of your life close to Him. You know His voice and can decipher when it is Him speaking or not. When we love the Lord with all our soul we can smile to ourselves when we know it is He who is working in our life and on our behalf. This is when we can praise the Lord and sing "Bless the Lord, oh my soul and all that is within me, bless His holy name".

All your mind:

Our minds can be occupied with many things on any given day. Often I would find myself unable to turn my thoughts off. I would find that I would dwell on a situation replaying it over and over in my head. Eventually those thoughts turn into worry or stress. It was during these times that I knew I needed to be in a place of stillness and meditation.

In Chapter 17 we spoke about being mindful of our thoughts and here we are talking about pleasing the Lord with our thoughts and the things we meditate on. In the Bible, when Joshua was chosen as Moses' successor, to lead the children of Israel to the promised land, the Lord understood the task he was to face. He knew the pitfalls of Moses, which included distractions, frustrations, doubt and disobedience, and He wanted Joshua to avoid them. He directed him with these words in Joshua 1:8, "This book of the law shall not depart from your mouth, but you shall meditate on it day and night, so that you may be careful to do according to all that is written in it; for then you will make your way prosperous, and then you will have success."

Don't you find that thing you think most about you also talk the most about? So if you are going through a situation you constantly talk about it with people whether to vent or to seek a solution. When you are in a relationship with someone you often talk about them at every opportunity you can. When we love God with all our mind we are constantly thinking about the goodness and grace and mercy He has given to us in our lives. When we read the word, we can rest on His word when we find ourselves going through situations. But it mustn't end there. If we love Him, He wants us to share that with others. If we are the only Bible some people may read, what are we telling them? Throughout the Bible, we see many examples of people running to tell of the goodness of God. Romans 10:17 states, "So faith comes from hearing, that is, hearing the Good News about Christ." It is for us to share the word for others to hear. We are reminded in Romans 10:14, "But how can they call on him to save them unless they believe in him? And how can they believe in him if they have never heard about him? And how can they hear about him unless someone tells them?" That someone is you, that someone is me.

Our worship through our heart, soul and mind can be summed up with a spirit of thanksgiving and worship. "You must fear the Lord your God and worship him and cling to him…" (Deuteronomy 10:20). Psalm 100, written as a hymn of praise and thanksgiving, is one of many that demonstrates how we can show our love toward God:

[1]Shout with joy to the Lord, all the earth!
[2]Worship the Lord with gladness.
Come before him, singing with joy.
[3]Acknowledge that the Lord is God!
He made us, and we are his.
We are his people, the sheep of his pasture.
[4]Enter his gates with thanksgiving;
go into his courts with praise.
Give thanks to him and praise his name.
[5]For the Lord is good.
His unfailing love continues forever,
and his faithfulness continues to each generation.

AN ENCOURAGER

CHAPTER 22

Proverbs 31:31

"Reward her for all she has done. Let her deeds publicly declare her praise."

I AM...
AN ENCOURAGER

This final verse exudes, screams, shouts women empowerment. I see all the tag lines flashing before me: 'Girl Power,' 'Sisterhood,' 'Soul sisters.' This verse isn't suggestive, it's not a question and it's not a plea. It is a bold statement. It's a statement to the King to honour, recognize and lift up this woman for all she does and all she is.

Some women have several circles of friends. Those they pray with, those who support them unconditionally, those who are an emotional support to them and those who they just want to have a good laugh with. Some relationships develop from childhood, through work, church, mutual friendships or interests. Relationships are formed and broken throughout the course of life. You grow into some and outgrow others, but when you find solid, honest friendship and support, hold those close and nourish them as often as possible. The Bible has many examples of all different kinds of friendships. There is David and Jonathan who were best of friends until death. There was Job whose friends doubted him and turned against him during his time of testing. Then there is Jesus who had his inner circle and an even smaller circle of His selected few with whom He was extremely close. His circle supported him, followed him, protected him and encouraged him. They also doubted him, disappointed him and even turned their backs on him. But in all His wisdom, Jesus knew the hearts of His friends. He knew how they would treat Him and He knew to forgive them. He knew not everyone who shows up in our lives would always have the best interest for us. He wants us to use discernment with those who we bring close to us and who we share our visions and dreams with. We are to be nice but not naïve, wise and not weary. We can, however, be the one who rewards, encourages, supports, prays and shows up. It is not for us to question the works of our fellow sisters. It is not for us to question their gifts and the call on their life. Our role is to challenge one another for the better; that is, to enhance one another in truth and in spirit. That does not involve bringing our sisters down in order to lift ourselves up or manipulating a situation out of jealousy. Galatians 5:25 and 26 states, "Since we are living by the Spirit, let us follow the Spirit's leading in every part of our lives. Let us not become conceited, or provoke one another, or be jealous of one another."

As women, we need support and we need encouragement. We also need to be that support and be that encouragement to each other. We all have gifts that can be used in one way or another. Your gift will make room for you and there is room for everyone's gift to be shared and appreciated. What is key to achieving this is being secure enough with ourselves and acknowledge this, so we can support and bless one another. Romans 12 teaches us about living in harmony with each other, supporting each other and encouraging each other. It speaks of the importance of our gifts being used to enhance each other and the kingdom. We are reminded that no man is more important than the other as we are here to honour God for who He is and what He does for us and not for who we are and what we do for Him.

Romans 12 continues with the various ways we can encourage each other, whether through rejoicing and praising one another for our accomplishments, or showing empathy and compassion rather than gossiping and judging our sisters when they fall. We can take the time to understand each other and why our sister is the way she is. We never know what people went through or are going through. We don't need to tear each other down whether with our words, actions, silence or inactions. We don't need to be catty and resentful of one another. Our gifts will make room for each one of us and we have been assigned to a purpose that is not designed for anyone else. So, no one can block your purpose and your purpose will not block the call over anyone else. The prophet Jonah never learned this lesson.

When Jonah was directed by God to minister to the people of Nineveh, he refused to obey God. He was gifted as a prophet, but his heart became hardened when his focus switched from pleasing God with his gift, to judging a people and allowing his feelings and emotions to get the best of him. He outright refused to allow God to bless the people of Nineveh because of what he thought about them. He went through great lengths to block their blessing. He ran the other way, like how we can act when we pretend not to see people and turn the other way, refusing to speak to them, or show compassion, support and love. He cursed their name, like how we can talk about people without really knowing what God is doing through them. He became bitter when God blessed them like how we can become when we are jealous, unforgiving and revengeful of another's blessing. A Jonah spirit will test our true sisterhood and friendship. A Jonah spirit will keep you in spiritual bondage preventing you to be free to minister, pray, forgive, encourage, support and allowing your gift to fully flourish. A Jonah spirit will prevent you from loving others unconditionally. A Jonah spirit will negate your gift and all you do will be in vain. Without the love of God, we would 'be nothing' and we 'would have gained nothing' (1 Corinthians 13:1-3) ultimately stifling the growth of the kingdom.

"It's not important who does the planting, or who does the watering. What's important is that God makes the seed grow. The one who plants and the one who waters work together with the same purpose. And both will be rewarded for their own hard work." (1 Corinthians 3:7-8)

Let's create real sisterhood remembering there is room for every woman to win!

2 Corinthians 13:11 "…Be joyful. Grow to maturity. Encourage each other. Live in harmony and peace. Then the God of love and peace will be with you."

Biography

Carla George is the founder of the Date Night! Series and has a passion for building solid Godly marriages to build strong families and communities. She does this by bringing together and hosting couples on community date nights. In her island home of Bermuda she has served on many government boards and currently sits as a Human Rights Commissioner. She has also served in several capacities in her church, Mt Zion AME Church. She has been a Steward for over 10 years and heads up the Visual Ministry. She has spent over 15 years in the corporate world in insurance and as a corporate lawyer. She and her husband of two years, a gift from God, Marcus (DJ Chubb) George reside in Bermuda with their boxer dog Café, but are citizens of the world with their love for travel and people!

Carla has been through various life obstacles that only God could pull her through. She calls these her character building moments and considers her life a testimony. Psalm 71:7 is a reminder of where she has come from and encourages her to live her life as an example of hope to many others:

"My life is an example to many, because you have been my strength and protection."

Carla has provided additional stretch exercise programs that co-ordinate with this book. You can access them on her website www.iamcarlageorge.com or email her at iamcarlageorge@gmail.com.

You can also reach her on Instagram @iamcarlageorge.

50901025R00088

Made in the USA
San Bernardino, CA
30 August 2019